Quest from the West

A Journey to the 2012 Little League World Series

Alexie Buhrer

DEDICATION

This book is dedicated to my son, Blake Buhrer, who proved to me baseball is magical.

CONTENTS

ACKNOWLEDGMENTS

This is the section where I thank folks who in some way contributed to this book. There are so many people and organizations to thank, so this is my short list.   You can skip this section if you think you're not in it, but I recommend reading through it just in case.

In San Bernardino, CA, thanks to:
- The staff at the Hampton Inn in Colton, California for their gracious support of the team and the red glitter cleanup
- Rico's Tacos, across the parking lot from the Hampton Inn, in Colton, California for their amazing $1.60 tacos

In Williamsport, PA, thanks to:
- Kathy at the Genetti hotel for the room upgrade
- Mark at the Genetti hotel for the generous and grand team party
- The bar staff at the Genetti hotel for their attentiveness and support
- The strangers who attended the games and wore bright yellow West gear in support of the Petaluma boys.

Thanks to my friends:
- Donna Woods, Blake's godmother, for supplying trail mix
- The Stoll, Jacobs and Costa families for understanding why we had to skip the camping trip
- Mike, Cassie, Sam, and Stella Jacobs for coming along for the ride to San Bernardino and Williamsport
- Melanie Muir for taking care of our precious cats while we were in Williamsport and checking in with Bailey
- Josie Nowak for taking care of our precious cats while we were in San Bernardino
- Tami Freitas who reminded me that "good things happen to good people" and for feeding Bailey
- Susan Hamilton for collecting articles about the team from the local newspapers

In Petaluma, CA, thanks to:

- All twelve sets of parents from the West team who welcomed the Buhrer family into their own
- Troy Sanderson for making sure we understood the expense boundaries
- Becky Smith for instructions on the Huddle
- Nicole Marzo for supporting the reprint of the All-Star T-shirts
- Jon Banister for suggesting I write this book
- Tina Stephens for running at my speed
- Eric Smith, manager of the boys, for the 10:15pm call and his magnificent coaching skills
- Mike Slate, team coach, for reminding Blake to call and text home

In the greater Petaluma community, thanks to:

- All the team fans for their generous financial assistance and undying support
- Sue, from Petaluma Junior High, for helping with parent paperwork and sending the boys' school schedules via email
- Matt Cain, pitcher for the San Francisco Giants, for calling the team in Williamsport and talking to each player individually, then following through on the promise to host a pizza party
- Jonny Gomes, designated hitter for the Oakland A's, for remembering what it was like growing up in Petaluma, posting his constant support of the team on social media, attending the community celebration, and hosting the boys at the A's game when they returned home

My family, thanks to:

- My Mom, Helen, for being Blake's good luck charm
- My Daughter, Bailey, who gave up her camping trip, her birthday celebration, and so many other things to honor her brother

- My husband, Bob, for helping me with the facts in this book, and telling me I look good in yellow
- My son, Blake, for taking us on this amazing journey

1 - INTRODUCTION

This book was written upon my family's return from the Little League World Series in Williamsport, PA in 2012. My son, Blake Buhrer, played on the West team during the series. I did NOT plan on writing a book about our experiences so I did not keep notes along the way. Forgive me if my facts are a little off, or the timing described in my story is vague.

The book idea was triggered by one of the team parents, Jon Banister, after one of our Williamsport games. He said to my husband and I, "Do either of you write?" My husband said, "Yea, Alexie does. She is in the middle of writing her first book right now."

Jon responded, "Good. You might want to tell your family's story, it is pretty incredible."

I spent a few days thinking about it. I threw together an outline, put the draft of my other book aside and starting writing this book two days after our return from Williamsport.

Hopefully this book inspires you to take the trip of a lifetime to experience a bunch of 12 year old boys and girls playing the world's largest organized youth sport. If it does not inspire you to take the trip, I hope it inspires you to follow the Little League World Series, because there is definitely something magical about watching a bunch of kids playing the game they love, in front of millions of viewers, without regard for anything but a small white ball with red stitching. Simple as that.

One final note, I am not a writer. I am just a parent. The writing in this book is less than professional, but it is how I would express myself if I were telling you this story, in person, over a glass of good red wine.

2 - 2012 PETALUMA NATIONAL LITTLE LEAGUE SEASON

January Baseball signups

Back in January, 2012, I downloaded the forms from the Petaluma National Little League (PNLL) site, completed them, found my most current utility bill and drove off to sign up my son for his final year in the Majors (term for 10, 11 and 12 year old players). For those of you that are not Little League parents, you have to bring your utility bill for proof of residence. The teams are formulated based on where you live. This is to make sure the team composition is reasonably fair… no team "stacking."

There were two or three different in-person sign-up dates. But, being an experienced Little League mom, I had already figured out the best time to go to avoid long lines. In previous years, I learned NOT to go on the weekend. Tried that, and could not even find a parking spot. Then, when I finally got into the front door, it was a total social event, and I spent hours in there saying "Hi" to every baseball parent in town. So, my secret was to go during one of the week night sign-ups during the final hour. By then, the place was almost a ghost town except for the other parents, who like me, had figured out the optimal time slot.

I wrote my dues check, filled out a form that said I was not a criminal, approved of a background check so that I could volunteer at the snack

3

shack and I was done.   My 12 year old son, Blake Buhrer, was signed up.

All I could do now was hope for a good coaching staff. Through the years, we had some really great managers and some not-so- great managers. I was hoping for a great one. In general, a great manager is someone that passionately cares about the game, teaches the players, challenges them to improve, and sets the standard for good sportsmanship. An example of a not-so-great manager is the Dad thinking coaching is a way to connect with his own son, or even worse, the Dad who thinks coaching will improve his son's play time.

Also in January, Blake made a significant decision, for a 12 year old. He had played baseball for years. He had also been pursuing his black belt in Tae Kwan Do since he was 7. He was one belt away from his black, when, to our dismay, he announced he wanted to quit Tae Kwan Do. To earn his black belt, he knew there was at least a year ahead of consistent practice, training and focus. Bob, Blake's father and my husband, and I do not raise quitters, so we had some long conversations around his decision, but in the end we supported it.   He had made a choice. We listened. Blake's passion was baseball, and he wanted to devote more time to it. Decision made, no black belt.

February

Last year, during my son's 11 year old Little League Season, he was on a winning team, sponsored by Pinky's Pizza. What I did not realize at the time, is when your child is on a winning team, you might as well kiss off any vacation plans you have for the month of June. But because of my ignorance, we had plans that summer to follow my teenage daughter, Bailey, on a school sponsored trip to France. So in 2011, as Blake's Pinky's team continued onto the City tournament, Blake had to leave to go to France. He was not happy. My explanation: I cannot make everyone happy all the time; I am the "Mother."

In 2012, we vowed to schedule our vacation properly and avoid planning anything until August just in case Blake's baseball team played well enough to move on. Four non-baseball families, plus the Buhrers,, had plans to go camping to our favorite camp site in early August. The special thing about this camping trip was it included my daughter's friends who were graduating from high school. This would be one of their last times together before they all left for college. And, as a bonus, the same families had children Blake's age. The plan was, kids and parents would enjoy fun, sun, boating, hiking and smores. To ensure we all had camp sites, we coordinated an online camp site registration at 8 am, exactly 7 months prior to our requested dates. It worked. We all had sites at the McArthur Park Burney Falls Camp Ground in Northern California, for the week of August 4, 2012.

March

We learned the names of our manager and coach. I think someone slipped us the information before the team manager called. I cannot remember exactly. As I said, we were hoping for a great manager and coaching staff. What we got was an unknown. We did not know the manager or the coach, so we were initially disappointed. We knew we wanted someone who would continue to help our son learn. We had no idea what to expect. The good news was there were a few other players on our team Blake had played with before including Quinton Gago and Logan Douglas. Blake was happy with the team composition. Bob and I were withholding judgment until the games started.

April and May

Practices were fine. Nothing spectacular, just the usual baseball practice stuff. The team sponsor was the Elks Lodge. The uniform was red. Ok, so far so good. Then, we played two games. Blake did not play the full games and was positioned in the outfield. I was not happy. My husband tried to calm me down by saying that Blake had missed some practices and I could not expect for Blake to be playing without being at practices. I agreed. Basic sport rule, if you miss practice, you cannot expect to play. However, that being said, I was not going to sit through yet another game without at least communicating my frustration to the coaching staff – in the nicest possible way. My opportunity came when I was walking toward the field with the coach. I had a frank conversation about Blake's play time and that my expectation was, since he was 12, he should get more playtime and play in the infield. The coach was kind, but seemed to respond in support of the manager and frankly, I felt sure I had royally pissed him off.

The next game, Blake played all 6 innings, in various positions in the infield, and that was the beginning of his role as a leading force on the team. I guess talking to the coach was an ok thing to do. Phew.

I am not sure when Blake hit his first homerun, but it was a doozie. My husband Bob and I were beyond excited. I did not even take a picture. I just stood up, screamed my lungs out, then looked at Bob and smiled. Bob left the stands to retrieve the homerun ball to start his son's homerun ball collection. As most father do, he writes a date on each home run ball, and lines them up on display on his workbench in the garage.

Later in the season, when Blake's grandmother was at the ballpark, Blake hit his first grand slam followed by a homerun. After that, he asked her to come to each game because she was his "good luck" charm.

After one of Blake's grand slams, we met up for dinner with a group of our friends, who are also baseball parents. When we announced Blake had hit a grand slam, they all give us big hugs. One parent said "you know what that means don't you?" We did not. He explained if your son hits a grand slam, you buy dinner. That was an expensive night. We did not fall for that costly trick on subsequent grand slams! Good thing because little did we know we needed to save our money for the next baseball adventure.

There is a Petaluma National Little League Website where, during the season, the league tallies the number of homeruns hit by each player. As the season progressed, Blake watched his homerun count increase. He relished batting cleanup, playing as an infield starter, and being a key contributor to the success of the team.

June – the First Half

The Elks team had a great season; they made it to the league championship game. In the weeks leading up to that game, there was a lot of talk in the stands, about the 12 year old Petaluma National All-Star Team selection. Every parent wants their child to make the team. And, many people voice their opinions about who will be selected. In Petaluma, the All-Star team is a hand selected collection of kids from across all teams in the league. They are considered the best of the best players. Blake had not made the All-Star teams in past years. He was a good player, but never good enough to be considered an All-Star. This year based on his performance, he was in the mix for consideration. But, there were factors that were not in his favor.

He had not been on the All-Star teams in prior years. He was on the Elk's team with two kids who would likely make the All-Star team (three All-Stars from one team is not common). Would they take three kids from the same team? Would they take 13 players onto the team or only 12? Would they stick with the same All-Star players from last year?

In Petaluma, voting for All-Stars works like this. For 12 year olds, each player in the league votes by selecting their top 8 All-Star picks for the All-Star teams. Then, all the coaches in the league meet, review the voting scores and add the remaining 4-5 players to the team based on their experience with the kids. There was no way to guess what the outcome. You just have to wait.

Bob and I heard many parent and coach comments on whether or not Blake would make the team. Parents from the Elks were sure that Blake was a shoo- in. Blake's batting coach told him he should be selected, but not to count on it because he had not been selected in the past, and he would have to "knock" someone off the roster to get on. He told Blake, "Don't be disappointed when you don't get selected. You played a good year." Everyone had input.

Bob and I did our best to stay neutral, and tried not to bring up the subject outside the house. At home, we attempted to set Blake's expectations around not making the team. Our thinking was that if he made it, it was a bonus, if he did not, at least we had prepared him.

All the while we were preparing for the league championship game. It would be the Elks versus a team from the Petaluma Valley league. Then, we found out the league would announce the members of the All-Start team the day before the championship game. Blake knew that on Friday, if the phone rang, it could be the All-Star coach calling for him. He sat home all day watching TV waiting. I called the house around 11am to check in with him, and he was very angry with me for tying up the line. I hung up and prayed the All-Star call would come.

At 4pm that day, his sister Bailey, took him to baseball practice, the final practice before the championship game. When he got there, Elk's team mates, Logan Douglas and Quinton Gago told him they had received the All-Star call. I am not sure how practice went, but I am sure it was the longest practice of Blake's life. When I picked him up, he told me we had to go home immediately in case a call came in for him. Privately, I texted another parent who was in the loop and asked if the All-Star calls were complete. She confirmed they were. I sat Blake down on the couch and with a lump in my throat, I laid out the painful truth. The calls were complete, the coach was not going to call him; he had not made the 12 year old All-Star team.

That was the beginning of the end for Blake. He cried like I have never seen anyone cry before. It was a combination of the sorrow of a man aching for something he had loved and lost, and the streaming tears of a toddler falling part because he could not have what he wanted. More tears than you can imagine. To his core, he was broken. My heart ached for him. He went upstairs crawled into his bed with his cats and cried for hours until he fell asleep for the night.

Whatever I said, whatever his dad said did not matter. By not being selected, his peers, coaches and managers had passively told him, "You are not good enough. You do not belong in this group. You are not part of this All-Star team."

The following day, we had the Elks championship game to play. Blake woke up with swollen eyes from hours of crying. I was sure he did not sleep well. Bob immediately texted the Elks team manager and told him Blake would likely not be on his game because he had learned he did not make the All-Star team the previous night. In a huge gesture of kindness and faith in my child, the Elk's manager put my son in as the starting pitcher in the championship game. His eyes were still swollen from crying. He walked to the mound after no fewer than five people asked him if he made All-Stars. His simple answer each time was "no." I was not sure how much more he could take. I knew the manager had made a mistake putting him in at starting pitcher. He had his game face on despite his swollen eyes and broken spirit, but he pitched the worse 2 innings of his baseball career. He was completely spent. He got pulled from the mound and put on third base to finish the game. The Elks lost. As we walked to the car, some of the All-Star players were getting fitted for their uniforms and signing the obligatory, participation paperwork in the parking lot. We could not walk by fast enough to hide the tears streaming down Blake's face.

The day was not over. Weeks before, Bob and I signed up to host the end of year Elks team party at our home. If only we had seen what was coming. No backing out now. We tried to convince ourselves the party would be a good distraction for Blake, and it was.

All the Elk's team families attended. The kids played whiffle ball, basketball, football, ping pong and used the batting cage in the garage. The adults relaxed, ate good food, drank beer and reminisced about the season. At the party, at least two parents expressed their sympathies to Bob and I about Blake not making the All-Star team. Bob and I just smiled, not knowing what to say.

June - the Second Half

The second half of June was torture for the entire family. Blake was not showing any signs of emotional recovery. He was cantankerous, and inconsolable. One day, he woke up and said, "I am not going to watch any of the All-Star games. I just can't."

Another time, Bob said, "Let's go play catch," Blake answered, "Dad, I don't know if I will pick up another baseball again." He was serious. We were worried.

Blake became a couch potato for two weeks. He stopped using the batting cage, stopped contacting his friends. He stayed up late, slept in late, watched TV and played video games. Blake was going to start junior high school in the fall, and he was in no mental condition to step into a new environment and be successful. I encouraged him to call his friends and go to the movies or the local summer fair. His response was "all my friends are at baseball practice."

On one of my retail therapy sessions, I found a St. Christopher medal that had the saint on one side, and on the other side was a baseball player. I bought it for Blake and gave it to him to try to cheer him up. I told him when his baseball travel-ball season started up in the fall, he could wear it for good luck. He tried it out, wore it for one day, and then I found it on the kitchen table. He said he did not like wearing it because when he worked out, it stuck to his skin. I took it and told him I would wear it for him at his next baseball game. I was secretly wishing I was wearing it to his All-Star games.

One night, I went to the wine bar with two friends who are also baseball moms and whose sons both made the All-Star team. I turned to them both and explained my worries about Blake and asked for any input they might have. They were kind and understanding, but they could not offer any advice for Blake's condition. They both acknowledged the situation was a baseball parent's nightmare.

The one bright light we had was that in early August, before the start of the school year, we would be going on our camping trip with non-baseball families. Our hope was the camping trip would get his mind off of baseball. Thank goodness we booked the camping trip in January.

July – the 4th

On the Fourth of July, we celebrated at a BBQ with several baseball families. Each boy had on a bright red shirt with the Petaluma All-Star Logo on the front, and the team members' names listed on the back. Ouch. When it was time to go out for fireworks, each boy grabbed their red sweatshirt that matched their red All-Star shirt and put them on before going outside. Double ouch. I said nothing, did nothing, and tried to pretend Blake would not notice. Who was I kidding?

July – the 5th

Bob and I were in bed when the phone rang at 10:15pm. Because we have a teenage daughter, and she was out at a friend's house, I jumped to answer the phone with a bit of an adrenaline rush hoping she was ok. The caller said, "This is Eric, can I come over and talk with you and Bob?" I asked, "Right now?" He said "Yes." I was sleepy and perplexed, but I agreed.

The caller, Eric Smith, lives with his wife Becky and their two children, Hance and Indya, about a ¼ mile from us. Their family was also at the party on the Fourth of July and I suspected something went down there, maybe with the kids, and they wanted to come to talk about it. Eric also happened to be the All-Star manager of the 12 year olds, but neither Bob nor I considered the visit was about baseball. We put on our sweats, headed downstairs and waited for Eric's arrival.

Eric and Becky came to the front door. They must have known we were concerned because the first thing Eric said was, "Nothing is wrong."

I said, "You could have told me that on the phone!" He laughed. We proceeded into the kitchen and each of us took a spot around the kitchen island. Bob and I were very tense and serious. We were still unsure of why Eric insisted on coming for a visit on a Thursday night at 10:15.

Eric asked if Blake was home. I said he was, but he was upstairs and out of earshot. The rest is kind of a blur. Eric told us he was here because he wanted to offer the 13th spot on the 12 year old All-Star team to Blake. He explained one of the kids had quit the team and as the manager, he had the choice to either continue with 12 players, or add another player to the roster. He wanted to offer the 13th spot to Blake. If Blake did not take it, he would not fill it. He assured us Blake had earned the right to be on the team, and in fact, should have been on the team from the outset.

Bob and I were very quiet. We were standing on opposite sides of the kitchen island. I wanted to squeeze his hand or something, but he was not close enough. I considered winking, but I did not want to expose my complete and overwhelming giddiness at this amazing news. Eric went on to explain each child on the team is a starter and this would be an adjustment for Blake. He would not be a starter and would not get a lot of play time, (likely one at bat and two innings in the field). I asked Eric a few questions. I pinched myself. I heard words, but was not listening. I was screaming up and down with joy inside, already anticipating how Blake would take the news. In the end, Eric explained, with our support, he would like to call Blake tomorrow and offer him a spot on the team. Bob and I told him we were very grateful and Blake would be looking forward to his call. In 10 minutes, the Smiths were there and gone and Bob and I were left with a decision. Do we tell Blake now, or wait for morning. Duh…… We went right to his room.

Blake was in his bed listening to music. Bob motioned to him to take off his headphones. In a firm, mom-like voice I said you had better get to sleep. He said "Why, it's the summer?"

I said "Because Eric and Becky just left the house and you have a spot on the All-Star Team. You have practice tomorrow."

In that moment, our son transformed back into the boy we raised. He scrambled out from under his covers and said "What?" We told him the whole story. No one in the Buhrer house slept well that night thanks to Eric Smith.

On July 6, Blake took the call from Eric and graciously (as gracious as a 12 year old boy can be) accepted the position on the team. Our son was back. He could not wait to get his glove on.

A few days later Becky told me she and Eric got into an argument the night they came by the house. Apparently, Eric did not want her to accompany him. Becky and I are friends, and Eric was afraid if she tagged along, it gave the impression of informality. He wanted to be clear he was there as a manager, not as a friend. Becky won the argument (sort of). She promised to sit in the car when Eric came over, but when they arrived, she followed along into the house. And so now you have a glimpse into the relationship between Eric and Becky. Both are clever, sensitive and driven. And, they both truly have great respect for the players, parents, and the game of baseball.

3 - 2012 PETALUMA NATIONAL ALL-STARS

The 13 Amazing Boys on the 2012 Petaluma National All-Star Team

Kempton Brandis
Blake Buhrer
Logan Douglas
Quinton Gago
Danny Marzo
Dylan Moore
James O'Hanlan
Austin Paretti
Porter Slate
Hance Smith
Bradley Smith
Cole Tomei
Andrew White

The Skilled Managing and Coaching Staff

Eric Smith – Manager
Mike Slate – Coach
Trevor Tomei – Coach

The Huddle

Within hours after Blake became an official team member, Becky Smith texted me and said now that Blake is on the team, Bob and I should join the "Huddle." The Huddle is a group text whereby all the parents of the team can communicate. I am all about being in the loop and communicating. I registered for the Huddle immediately. We just had to respond to a text from the Huddle, and we were in. Immediately after we joined the Huddle, the texts started coming at us from other parents welcoming our family to the team. We were touched.

Special note to inexperienced Huddle users….. There is definitely Huddle etiquette. Becky cautioned me about the Huddle. Don't send messages to the Huddle on accident, it could prove to be embarrassing. I guess last year someone accidently sent a message to the Huddle about a drunken baseball mom they spotted at the fair. Not good. Got it, be careful when texting to the Huddle. I will just say right now, after my experience with this technology, some people definitely need to take Huddle lessons. The Huddle is a great method for communicating and an even greater method for embarrassing yourself!

District Championship: June 30-July 9

The team had been practicing for over two weeks without Blake. He went to his first practice, did well defensively, but was a wreck at the plate. He was very nervous and frankly had not touched a ball since the loss at the Elks championship game. Time to order up some one-on-one time with Blake's batting coach. Blake was assigned jersey number 22. I liked that number. During the regular season he had jersey number 12, it seemed fitting that in the All-Stars he was 22, ten points more important (just a mom overthinking).

Blake had also missed a few of the All-Star games. The day after Blake's first practice, the team was playing the final District All-Star Championship game against Petaluma Valley. The winner of this tournament would move onto the Section Championships. I put on Blake's St. Christopher medal. My fingers memorized the medal as I rubbed it when he came to bat. Petaluma Nationals lost the game, however, the tournament was not over. The Petaluma Valley team was strong, but they had to beat Petaluma National twice in order to move on since our winning record in the tournament was better than theirs. We had to play them one more time, and the winner of the next game would move on. I was not concerned, I

14

was still so elated that we were there. Blake was happy and playing ball again.

Back again on Monday night to play Petaluma Valley again for the District Championship. We won the game. The boys were presented with the District Championship banner, the local press and every team parent took pictures. I think there was a small article in the paper about the success of the team, nothing splashy, just local sport news.

District Championship Results – June 30-July 9

Win: Petaluma National Little League (PNLL) 14, Santa Rosa American 0

Win: Petaluma National Little League (PNLL) 10, Petaluma Valley 0

Win: Petaluma National Little League (PNLL) 19, Petaluma American 9

Win: Petaluma National Little League (PNLL) 14, Ukiah, 4

Loss: Petaluma Valley 8, Petaluma National Little League (PNLL) 7

Win: Petaluma National Little League (PNLL) 13, Petaluma Valley 1

Emails from Eric (Team Manager)

July 9, 2012

Hi Everyone,

Congratulations to the boys. Remember their faces as they ran around the field today after the game. That's always fun to see.

Here is the schedule for this week:

Tuesday - off
Wednesday - 5:00 - 7:00
Thursday - 5:00 - 7:00
Friday - at the barn 4:00 - 7:00
   4:00 - 4:30 - Porter, Bradley, Dylan
   4:35 - 5:10 - Quinton, Hance, Logan,
   5:15 - 5:50 - Andrew, Cole, Austin
   5:50 - 6:30 - Blake, Danny, Kempton

Saturday - Gameday - 1:00, arrive by 11:30, Park information is available now at
http://www.eteamz.com/llbcaliforniadistrict35/files/LittleLeagueSection2012.pdf

I would like to have a short parent meeting before Wednesday's practice, starting at 4:45. It'll take 10 minutes.

Let me know if you have any questions.

Eric

July 10, 2012

I need to redo the Friday barn schedule.

4:00 - 4:40 - Danny, Blake, Dylan, James
4:40 - 5:10 - Bradley, Quinton, Logan
5:15 - 5:45 - Andrew, Cole, Austin
5:50 - 6:20 - Kempton, Hance, Porter

Sorry for any inconvenience.
Eric

The barn is really a barn. It has been set up as a giant, well equipped batting cage. The boys utilize the barn as often as they can courtesy of Jon Banister, Porter's mother's boyfriend. In addition to regular baseball practice, it is a given that each player spends additional time practicing their swing and improving their batting skills. The barn was yet another resource for the players to refine their talent. I remember one time, over dinner, Blake told us he had spent some time at the barn with Jon. Jon said to him "nice swing," he paused for a second or two and followed with "for a four year old." We laughed. Blake went on to say Jon helped him improve his swing and he assured us he did not really swing like a four year old. We already knew that, but I guess he felt like he had to tell us.

Section Championships: Fairfield – July 14-19

Following the District Championship, the next tournament for the Section Championships was scheduled for July 14-19 in Fairfield, California. It was to be played as double elimination. For non-baseball folks, that means if you lose twice you are out of the tournament. If you lose once, you play in the loser's bracket and can still get to the championship game, but you have to play more games to get there. No one wants to play in the loser's bracket. I guess that's pretty obvious.

The plan was to meet at Starbucks on Saturday morning so we could car pool or caravan to the tournament. I guess this was standard practice for the team. Ok, we were in. See you at Starbucks.

The Bright Red Shirts

During the week prior to the Fairfield tournament, Nicole Marzo (Danny 's mom), told me the league board members had met and voted to reprint the bright red t-shirts and sweatshirts for the team. The reprints would include Blake's name. Wow. She knew the significance of the shirts. I wanted to tell her how much it meant to Blake, but she clearly got it. I did not tell Blake about the shirts. I wanted to wait until I could hand him one.

On Saturday morning, Nicole texted me that the shirts and sweatshirts were ready for pickup. I could not even come up with the words to explain to her how much this meant to Blake. I just hugged and thanked her. It did not seem like enough, but I did not want to overdo it.

Blake was still in his bed when I brought the new red shirts into the house. Bob put on his own and walked into Blake's room. He turned around and showed Blake the team list on the back. Blake was quiet. He got out of bed and put on his own red shirt. The front said Petaluma National Little League All-Stars, the back said his name. He was where he belonged. It was official, he was part of the team. He proudly wore the shirt en route to the Fairfield tournament, just like the other 12 players.

Teddy Tradition

Somewhere along the way in this tournament, Bob and I learned about the "Teddy Tradition." Teddy Belove is a young boy with a cherub-like face, his older brother plays as an 11 year old Little Leaguer. I am not sure how the tradition started, but I did not question it. Rub Teddy's golden locks before each game for good luck. If Teddy was not available at the start of the game, then rub his hair in the picture posted in the dugout. Every player and every coach, period.

Besides the Teddy superstition, there were many other personal and private superstitions people developed on the journey. I don't know them all, but they were rampant.

When we were in San Bernardino, a woman sought out the three coach's wives. She handed them each collector pins shaped like colorful butterflies, and said she had hand made them, and they were good luck. Becky turned over her butterfly pin and it said "made in China." Were the pins bad luck? Was this woman sincere, or were the pins cursed? Becky and the other two moms wore the pins for an inning or two, and our team fell behind in the score of the game. Collectively, we decided the pins had to go. Sonny, Quinton's father, gathered the pins, and had his youngest boys hide them under the opponents seats. We turned the game around after the butterflies were secretly planted. From that game forward, prior to each game, the Gago brothers would inconspicuously re-position the pins in the opponent's stand, then collect them when the games were over. We lost track of the pins when we headed for Williamsport, but we felt sure the butterfly ritual had contributed to the team's success in San Bernardino.

Once we got to Williamsport, Bob insisted on wearing his orange Calvin Klein boxers to every game. I spent way too much time in the hotel laundry facility to support that superstition. I, on the other hand, became fixated on my on-loan St. Christopher medal. Mostly, no one talked about their superstitions outside of their own families. But I would put money on it each family had at least one.

The Tournament and Fans
The Fairfield field was nice. It was about an hour drive from Petaluma. The weather was perfect for baseball. The fan base from our hometown was impressive. We had a sea of red shirts in the stands watching every game. More fans showed up for the weekend games than the week night games, but still an amazing showing of support for the boys.

Blake's and Bailey's godparents lived near Fairfield, California, so they were there for every game. Whatever was happening in their non-baseball lives was put aside, and they were hooked. It was amazing watching them transform into seasoned fans. They started out as newbies in the stands, and within two games, they knew all the players names, the parents of each player and had mastered the team cheers. Two more devoted fans!

I asked Blake what the rest of the team thought about the tournament competition. He said the team felt that every game was going to be a challenge. I was glad to hear the coaching staff had made it clear every game mattered and every team was going to come to win.

The big competitive surprise in the tournament was the Vacaville, California team. We faced them in our second game. Vacaville was comprised of several boys that were Blake's size. Bigger is not always better, but it can sometimes be intimidating. In addition, the team had some very strong pitching. Not one good pitcher, but at least three were throwing hard and over the plate.

At one point during the tournament, we arrived before our game and the boys had not eaten yet. I went to the snack bar and ordered 10 cheese burgers. The grill was not on yet, but the marvelous volunteer staff jumped to light the grill and prepare food for our players. Later that day, I thanked the gentleman who was barbequing. He said he was happy to get the burgers going for the boys. He went on to say the Petaluma parents and fans were such a nice group and he was happy to make a special effort for us since we were so polite. How nice! This was the first time, and there were many more, I felt proud to be part of the parent and fan base of the Petaluma team.

The Games

In our first game against Vacaville, we were down in the 6th. There were two outs, and two strikes against Danny Marzo. Danny hit a walk off homerun. The crowd went nuts! When the boys shook hands with the Vacaville team after the game, the Vacaville pitcher shared some foul words and gestures, and the coach was less than cordial. The rest of the Vacaville team was very respectful. Too bad, in my book, poor sportsmanship can lead to bad karma.

The Vacaville team dropped into the loser's bracket, but continued to play and win. They faced us again in the championship game. Petaluma won 10 to 1. Karma? Perhaps.

Blake performed well in the series. He had one at bat in the first 3 games, and two at bat in the final game. He walked, struck out, then had a double and two singles. He was contributing. I kept rubbing my St. Christopher medal. I guess I should say, I kept rubbing his St. Christopher medal I had on loan.

Section Championship Results

Win: Petaluma National Little League (PNLL) 14, LLL 4

Win: Petaluma National Little League (PNLL) 8, Vacaville Central 7

Win: Petaluma National Little League (PNLL) 9 San Francisco, American 4

Win: Petaluma National Little League (PNLL) 10, Vacaville Central 1

Emails from Eric (Team Manager)

July 20, 2012

Hi All,

Currently the plan is to be at the field at 10:30 in Fresno. The host district is providing a BBQ after the two games played at noon. I can only assume that the ceremony will be at this time.

The address for the field is:

Gomes Elementary School

503 Lemos Ln.

Fremont, CA 94539

This is District 14, although I have not seen any information on that site to this point. We have a coaches meeting tonight, and I will get you more information at that time if relevant.

Let's Go PNLL!

Eric

Author's note: Eric received a lot of emails back teasing him about the "Fresno" typo in his email dated July 20, 2012.

Division Championships: Fremont – July 21-28

Off to Fremont, not Fresno, for the Division Championships. The team met at Starbucks. I wore my on-loan St. Christopher medal. Bob, Bailey and I put on our red shirts. Blake's Godparents and the Petaluma fans were there for support.

Fremont was also a nice venue, about one and a half hours from Petaluma. It had two fields, and an "award winning" snack bar. Not sure it really was award winning, but the announcer assured us it was, multiple times. The tournament had a formal opening ceremony. The announcer who ran the ceremony started off by saying any one of these teams might end up in Williamsport, but for sure one of them will end up in San Bernardino. He had no idea then, but he was right on both accounts.

We won our first game against Turlock. At one point during that game, Becky Smith, Hance's mom, left the stands and went to use the restroom. While she was gone, her son hit a homerun. For the remainder of the tournament, we sent Becky to the bathroom whenever Hance was up to bat. While it sounds like a ridiculous behavior, it proved to be good luck. Hance hit more than his share of homeruns in the tournament, and Becky missed watching each one, but she understood it was for the good of the team. She could hear the cheers from the bathroom. That was good enough.

Blake, not unlike all other twelve year old boys, is somewhat obsessed with electronics. When it was time for him to get a cell phone, we gave him one of Bailey's old ones. It was a durable, basic phone he could use if he needed to text or call home. But, he was clearly in envy of all of his friends who had iPhones. He was saving his money to buy one on his own. One afternoon on our drive to Fremont, Blake said to Bob, "Hey Dad, if the team goes all the way to Williamsport, will you buy me an iPhone?" Bob, quickly responded with, "Sure." In light of the odds on getting to Williamsport, that answer was perfect.

Email from Eric (Team Manger)

July 21, 2012

Sunday game time is at 2:00 pm. The boys should be there at 12:30

ready to start warming up. We are scheduled to play on Field 1 tomorrow. We will meet at 10:40 at Starbucks on Lakeville for anyone who wants to carpool down.

Nice job by the boys today. It was good to get a game, and the jitters that go with that, out of the way.

Get 'em to bed early, and tell them I said "prepare like champions" (sleep well, eat well, and drink plenty of water.)

See you tomorrow. Let's go PNLL.

Eric

PS. More line drives and the homeruns will happen.

Game number two was against San Ramon. Parents, coaches and players told Bob and I about the rivalry between San Ramon and Petaluma. Apparently, in the two prior years during All-Star playoffs, the two teams battled fiercely. Petaluma won once, and San Ramon won once. This final tournament rematch would be the "winner" of the three year battle. We won the first game against them, sending San Ramon into the loser's bracket. We figured they would work their way through the loser bracket and we would play them again in the tournament championship game.

The San Ramon team exhibited good sportsmanship during the handshake at the end of the game. However, I cannot say the same about their parents and fans. At one point, late in the game, Austin Paretti came to the plate. Austin is one of Petaluma's smallest players. Never underestimate small. He was batting in the 8th spot in the order. A fan from the San Ramon side, hollered to the pitcher, "You can get this guy, he's the 8th batter." Bob and I looked at each other in disgust. What a stupid, rude, and mean thing to holler! If that guy was in our crowd we would have been totally embarrassed. I am not sure if Austin heard the idiot, but he swung the bat and smashed a homerun. I turned to Bob and whispered in his ear "And that was our 8th batter. Take that you dumb ass." Sorry for the bad word, but the situation warranted it.

Email from Eric (Team Manger)

July 23, 2012

Hi Everyone,

Great and exciting game on Sunday. Now on to the next. I want the kids to start thinking about what they have to do in their next game.

Monday - No practice

Tuesday - practice from 4:00 - 5:30 at Carter Field.

The Wednesday game begins at 5:00 (we play winner of Lakeside and River Park). Once again, because of traffic, I will encourage everyone to leave early. I will send another e-mail to confirm Wednesday's schedule.

Please continue to get the kids plenty of sleep so they are not recovering on game day. Sleepovers are fine, but they should still get to bed early. (I realize I may come off as crazy writing that last sentence.)

Thank you for all of your help.

Go PNLL,

Eric

July 23, 2012

Hi Everyone,

Mike and I drove down to Fremont this evening and it took us an hour and twenty minutes taking the 680 route. We left at 3:20. I would like everyone at the field ready to start hitting at 3:30, so we will meet at Starbuck's at 1:45, leaving at 2:00.

We will play River Park. They looked good tonight in their victory over Lakeside, so it will be another tough game. "Play like champions," and the boys will be fine. Please make sure the kids are fed on the way down so they are ready to go when they arrive. It will be awhile before we get a chance to get them fed.

Just so you know, it did start to cool down toward the end of the game tonight.

Please let me know if you have any questions.

Go PNLL,

Eric

We played game number three against River Park. It was well attended, and the boys hit and fielded well. The River Park Team (from the Fresno area) was a nice group of boys. Blake had two hits in the game, a double and a single. At that point, he was 4 hits for 5 at bats in the tournament.

It was time for the championship game on Friday night. Frankly, as a parent, I was really looking forward to this Friday night game. My thinking was…. win this game tonight, secure the championship and get the WHOLE weekend at home getting caught up on life. It was not to be. The crowd was huge. The Petaluma stands had a full-house, there were red t-shirts everywhere.

The San Ramon boys came to win. The game was close, but we lost in the final inning. Because we came from the winners bracket, San Ramon had to beat us twice to win the tournament. Our team was disappointed, but not defeated. They took it in stride and were ready to take on San Ramon one final time on Saturday. I was not looking forward to commuting back to Fremont, but I was surely not going to miss the final game. Based on the history between the San Ramon and Petaluma National team, I think we all had a feeling it would be epic. We were right.

The final game against San Ramon on Saturday did not have as big of a crowd as Friday night. I think some of the Petaluma fans had weekend plans. Imagine that, having plans outside of baseball. Too bad, because in my opinion, they missed the most thrilling baseball game the team has ever played. It is so unfortunate the game was not televised, because it was epic. I don't want to take anything away from the game that we played in Williamsport against Tennessee where Petaluma team scored 10 runs in the bottom of the 6th, but the reason I consider this game even more thrilling was that there was a comeback, a fall behind and a comeback. And we ultimately won. I will repeat myself, "simply epic." If you were there, you know. If you weren't, I am sorry you missed it.

I will try to recap the game, but I am sure my writing will not capture the extreme emotional highs and lows we experienced as parents and fans. The San Ramon team was up 8 to 1 in the 5th inning. We could hear their parents talking about how to get to San Bernardino, hotel arrangements and travel plans. I sat in the stands silent. I was thinking about what a great run we had had and how next week, we would leave to go on the camping trip we planned in January. I was thinking Blake should be happy, and proud of himself, for participating on the team.

Then, in the bottom of the fifth, our boys came alive. And, I mean alive like a bunch of well-trained athletes hungry for a win. There was no desperation, just total focus. Hit after hit, run after run, we tied the game at 8-8. The Petaluma crowd was wild with excitement. The San Ramon crowd was quiet. The momentum had shifted. The energy was amazing. In the stands, we were laughing and choking back tears of joy at the same time. We slapped each other on the back, gave high fives to our bleacher neighbors, cheered and chattered.

The game was not over. San Ramon came back to the plate and scored three runs. It was 11-8 in the bottom of the 6th. We had one final chance to score and win the game. I turned to Bob and Bailey and said "We are three outs away from our destiny. We are either going to San Bernardino or on our camping trip next week." They both looked at me and smiled. I was not sure which one they wished for, I knew where I wanted to go. I rubbed my on-loan St. Christopher medal and sat very, very still watching and waiting. The boys delivered. At the bottom of the 6th inning the game was tied again at 11-11. The game went into extra innings. There had to be a winner. There had to be a loser. Dylan Moore came to the mound to pitch to the top of the San Ramon order. He was nails. He shut down the inning and we went into the bottom of the 7th with a score of 11-11. San Ramon now had to pitch to the top of our order. The Petaluma boys did what they do best, hit. Hit 1, hit 2, hit 3. The bases were loaded. "Crack," Bradley Smith hit a hard ground ball to score Logan Douglas. GAME

OVER. Destiny determined. The Buhrer family was going to San Bernardino, the camping trip was officially cancelled.

Ok, so now I look around and I see Bob with tears in his eyes. I have only seen my husband cry a few times in 23 years of marriage, and I had to look away so as not to burst into tears myself. Then, I looked at the other folks in the crowd, and I see other fathers crying. I won't list their names here because they might be embarrassed if I write about their tears, but let me tell you there was a hell of a lot of proud parents out there overflowing with raw emotion.

The boys shook hands with the San Ramon team. Blake said the boys on the team were sad, but very polite. I cannot say the same about the parents or fans. I will leave it at that.

The Petaluma parents were escorted onto the field. The boys received their championship banner, ran around the field with it, and then joined the parents for 2,000 pictures, 4,000 hugs, 8,000 high fives. Ok, maybe I am exaggerating here, but it was a moment of champions.

Blake finished the tournament with 4 hits out of 7 at bats. Bob, Bailey and I were so happy for him.

According to the media, this was only the second time a team from Petaluma had ever won the Division Championship and been invited to San Bernardino. What an incredible accomplishment and honor.

Division Championship Results

Win: Petaluma National Little League (PNLL) 17, Turlock 0

Win: Petaluma National Little League (PNLL) 16, San Ramon 8

Win: Petaluma National Little League (PNLL) 15, River Park 0

Loss: San Ramon 8, Petaluma National Little League (PNLL) 7

Win: Petaluma National Little League (PNLL) 12, San Ramon 11

4 - WESTERN REGION
CHAMPIONSHIP – AUG 3-11

What's Next

How do we get there? How do the boys get there? When do we need to
go? Who pays for the trip? Where do we stay? All questions for which no
one had answers. Apparently, Eric had some San Bernardino paperwork he
had completely ignored until the final win. He did not want to read
anything about San Bernardino until he knew we were going. That would
be bad karma. Eric committed to reading through the paperwork and
filling us in.

On July 28, Jeff and Jackie, James's O'Hanlan's parents, hosted a potluck at
their home to celebrate, and provide a forum for Eric to tell us what was
next. The boys swam. The adults drank. Before everyone got too carried
away, Eric spoke. What he knew was brief. The league would provide a
very small amount of money per mile for transportation to San Bernardino.
The trip was approximately a 10 hour drive. The boys had to be on site at
the facility on Wednesday, August 1. They would need basic supplies like
clothes, a bathing suit, a toothbrush, a sleeping bag and their uniforms.
Laundry would be done on-site for the boys. They would each need a little
bit of spending money to buy souvenirs. Once they arrived, they would be
provided with a dorm like sleeping environment and all meals. On
occasion, based on game schedule and coach approval, parents would be
able to "check out" their kids for time away from the dorm/field. Oh, and

if parents arrived on Wednesday, they could tour the facility where the boys stayed, otherwise, parents would just have to use their imagination. It was so unlike Bob and I to nod our heads to the tidbits of information and not ask questions. But, we knew there was no more information, there was no time, and there was no need to expend energy on wondering. We would just have to follow and believe. Our first game was Friday evening, August 3.

Ok, what about accommodations and travel plans for parents and siblings? There was a list of recommended hotels in the area. A few of us pulled out our computers, but that night we could not come to a decision on where to stay, there was just too much celebrating going on. We tried, but each hotel we contacted did not have the right people on staff at 8pm on a Saturday night to help us with our room block dilemma.

The Ugly Day

The following day, July 29, Bailey and I were headed to Southern California (San Diego area) to visit some colleges she was interested in attending in the Fall of 2013. At the O'Hanlan BBQ the night before, I tried to stop drinking early so that our 6am flight would not be an ugly event for me. But, I got sucked into a shot of some god-awful sweet drink in the kitchen by Mereena Moore, Dylan's mom. The drink was prepared by her and Jackie, James' mom. I did not know either of them very well, and did not want to be insulting by refusing. I succumbed to the peer pressure and threw one back. After that, I knew I had made a mistake. I had Bob drive me and the family home immediately. The morning was going to be ugly. Damn....

Bailey and I got up at 4:30am and drove 30 minutes to the Santa Rosa, California airport to get on a plane. As predicted, I was feeling ugly. I had thought about cancelling the two day trip to Southern California once it was clear we were heading to San Bernardino. I thought we could just tour the colleges while we had breaks in between games. But I did not want to cancel because I did not want Bailey to think touring the colleges was not as important as her brother's baseball trip. We had already cancelled her camping trip! We got onto the plane. Did I mention I was feeling ugly? The stewardess went through the usual emergency exit spiel, and then just as we were getting ready to pull away from the gate, the pilot came onto the loud speaker and announced the plane was experiencing technical difficulties and would not be taking flight. We deplaned. At this point, I was still feeling awful. The airline explained they could bus us to San Francisco or Oakland for a flight, but that no other flight was available from that airport that day. Bailey turned to me and said "Mom, how far is San Bernardino from San Diego?" I told her it was about 2 hours, she said, "Let's just visit the colleges next week when we are down there." I love that kid. She is so wise, so selfless, so amazing. So, we cancelled our tickets, got a full refund, drove home and got back into bed by 8:30am. The ugly subsided.

That same day, Sunday, July 29, Nicole Marzo, Danny's mother, made the executive decision to book a block of rooms at the Hampton Inn in Colton, California. Thank goodness someone made a decision. Getting 13 families to come to agreement is no small task. Nicole has a knack for being decisive and taking charge. I appreciate her! The hotel was about a 15 minute drive to the field. In fact, every hotel in San Bernardino was about a 15 minute drive from the field, and there were not many choices. Decision made. The Buhrer family booked a room at the Hampton Inn in Colton and prepared for a trip to Southern California.

I talked to Becky Smith, Hance's mom, later in the day and confessed my "ugly incident." She and I pinkie promised there would be no more shots for either of us on the remainder of the journey. I was still feeling ugly enough to commit to the promise.

Email from Eric (Team Manger)

July 31, 2012
Hi All,

As of right now:

1. Practice at 4:00 - 5:30, Carter
2. We have a dine and donate set for BTG (Beyond the Glory, Sports Bar) Tuesday as a fundraiser, (mention Petaluma National Little League). I believe they will be showing some video from the championship game(s).
    - kids should wear hat and red All-Star shirt to BTG
3. We will be meeting Wednesday morning at Carter Field at 7:45 am.

      - KNBR at 8:02

      - decorate vehicles

4. Leave around 8:30 - 8:45, police escort to Novato

5. Box lunches donated, we may need a couple of coolers, but not sure how much space we have.

6. Laundry needs are donated, soap and change.

Other things:

Still working on getting games re-broadcast via radio/internet

Kids may want to pack a pillow

Let me know if you have any questions.

Go PNLL,

Eric

Departing from Petaluma's Carter Field

Wednesday, August 1st came fast. We marked Blake's clothes with his initials, packed his bag, sleeping bag and pillow and met at Carter Field at 7:45am. The meeting spot was significant. It was the new field the boys had played on during the standard little league season. It was also the field attached to Petaluma Junior High, the school that 12 of the 13 kids would attend in late August. As we approached the field, the gate for entry was decorated with streamers, homemade signs and toilet paper. It was a beautiful mess. To this day, I am not sure who put up the decorations, but it was such a wonderful site. At the field, there was a 15 passenger van waiting. Kailyn Paretti, Austin's sister, decorated the windows on the van with the Petaluma National Little League logo and words of good luck. The van was generously donated by a local company to get the team to and from San Bernardino. Ricardo Marzo, Danny's father, and Mike Smith, Bradley's father, followed the van in a truck full of the boys' bat and duffle bags.

Before the team pulled away from Petaluma Junior High, the kids loaded up on donuts, took a phone call from a local radio station to talk about the journey ahead and posed for local newspaper photographers. I think this was the first time the media began to play a role in the boys' baseball journey.

Bob and I were perplexed. We were used to packing up a pickup truck with a bunch of gear, sticking a bunch of kids in a car and heading out to play a game. Standard sport stuff. But, this attention from the media and the community was a bit startling. It seemed to make the boys a little more reserved, and the parents a little less expressive. I think we were all a bit afraid of getting our picture taken at an emotional moment.

The trip out of town included an escort by the Petaluma Police. Just before we were about to take off, I told some of the boys to gather up the players and go over to the police escorts and thank them by shaking their hands, but then the radio station phone call came in, so they missed their opportunity to personally say "thanks." After the call, they were ushered immediately into the van for their departure. There were two motorcycles cops, one police truck and at least one patrol card that lead the boys to the Sonoma County line. What a ride. A proud community moment.

Family Travel

Before I left town, I again needed to exercise some retail therapy. I scrambled to buy some red clothes. I found two shirts and called it good enough. Red was not a staple in my wardrobe. It is now.

Some families planned to fly, some families were going to drive, and the good news was that at least one parent for each child planned on heading to San Bernardino. There was some early community fund raising to help out with the financial strain for the parents and families. Before we left for San Bernardino trip, we received some funds toward our expenses. My family did not expect it, but we truly appreciated it.

Day 1: Friday, August 3

We flew into the Ontario, California Airport On Friday, August 3. It was 108 degrees when we landed. We rented a car, that Bailey named Suzanne, and made the short drive to San Bernardino. We stopped first at our hotel to check into our room, unload our luggage and get ready for the 4pm game.

When we arrived at the Hampton Inn in Colton, California, our room was not ready. But, the staff assured us that it would be available later in the

31

day. It was hot, we were cranky, but I accepted the information and we stuck our luggage in Becky Smith's room, and immediately left to go the field to check it out before game time.

The field was amazing. Not like a professional baseball field, but like a little league baseball field on steroids. It was built over 40 years ago and it was very well maintained. The seating capacity of 10,000 was so impressive. And, the place was buzzing with excited kids and families. We called Blake and he came out of his dorm to meet us. He was so happy, and excited. I could tell he had not slept well in days and he was running on pure adrenaline. I hoped that the boys would get over the newness of the "sleep over" for 13 and start getting to bed on time.

We returned to the hotel and our room was still not ready. I made the front desk promise we would have a room available after the game. There were so many folks checking in I was afraid our room would be given away while we were at the game. The hard working staff assured me our room would be waiting for us upon return from the game. Our room for the next 10 days would be 325. We scrambled to Becky's room where our luggage was being stored, put on our red fan wear and prepared for the 4pm game.

It was blazing by game time. The seats choices were either red plastic fold down chairs (traditional stadium seating), or large cement steps for "bleacher like" seating. Think giant cement steps about 4 feet deep. The red seats were hot because they were plastic and had back support that pressed my shirt against my sweaty back. The cement seats were hot because the cement was baking from the sun. We selected the red seats for the back support. We quickly got used to the familiar trickle of sweat dripping down our backs. But, it did not matter, once the game started, we stayed put.

As is the tradition, at the start of the game, we all stood to address the American Flag and sing the *Star Spangled Banner*. Somehow, standing at this new stadium, looking out at the flag that was lying still against the pole, I felt different. When I looked around, there were hundreds of people there, hundreds of people that I did not know. I wondered where they came from, and why they would come to watch strangers play baseball in 108 degree weather. While the sweat trickled down my back, I turned my eyes to the flag and begin to sing. As I sang, I experienced an emotional chill, which was strange since it was so hot. At that moment, I was really proud to be an American, about to sit down to watch America's favorite pastime. Then, I was jolted out of my "thankful to be an American moment" with a shout from the outfield by all the stadium volunteers in unison "PLAY BALL."

In our first game as Northern California in the Western Championships, we defeated Hawaii. They had a small, but enthusiastic fan base. They played a good game, but we played a better one.

Following the game was the opening ceremony for the West and Northwest Tournament. At the end of this tournament, two teams would be traveling to the Little League World Series, one representing the United States West, the other representing the United States Northwest. Each child held a balloon and one member of each team carried the state flag as the boys marched onto the field. What a sight. Then, upon command, the boys all released their balloons. The announcer explained the balloons signified each individual child, and letting them float away freely represented how the kids would intertwine as the week progressed. This same balloon ceremony was later repeated at the Little League World Series. The ceremony was visually amazing. At the time, I did not really hone in on the significance of the balloons and how they represented each child. But, as the journey continued, it became clear the boys, like the balloons rose and mixed together in an unpredictable, amazing way. Later I also realized it was a bittersweet message to me as a parent. It was time to let go and watch my child learn to find his way.

At the close of opening ceremony, the teams came into the stands and join with the parents for a "special surprise." As we watched, a helicopter landed on the field, spraying little pebbles of dirt into our eyes. A passenger got out of the helicopter and hand delivered baseballs to the league officials. When the helicopter took off again, we were smart enough to turn around to shield our eyes. The helicopter was a nice touch!

I cannot go on without making one small comment on the freeway system in Ontario, San Bernardino and Colton California. What a mess. Roadways were under construction or demolition. I was not sure which. The freeways were in some places barricaded to single lanes and there were little to no markings on exits or merges. Jeeze, a person could get lost in a place like this!

Day 2: Saturday, August 4

When we first learned of our bracket and game schedule, we were a bit disappointed, we had the first West game on Friday, and the remaining West teams did not have to play until Saturday. What we learned, however, was that our schedule was really an advantage. While we had to play first, later in the week, we would have a day off in the middle of the schedule to rest, where other teams would have games back to back.

On Saturday, August 4, we played Arizona at 11:30am. In Petaluma, we are not used to hot weather. Maybe 1 to 2 weeks out of the year, we get temperatures in the high 90's or low 100's. This place was literally as hot as hell. And, we had an 11:30 game in the baking sun. There were some make shift awnings over a small set of red chairs, however, if you sat under the awnings, the view was significantly restricted. I first sat outside the awning, then an hour into the game, I moved under. That was after I decided heat stroke was worse than having to contort my body underneath the awning to see where the ball landed.

We won the game. The boys returned to the barracks and jumped into the very inviting pool outside of their dorms. Through the fence, we watched them swim, then they came and greeted us for a few minutes of family time.

The parents returned to the hotel and began our own San Bernardino tradition of standing in the pool in a 10x12 foot shaded area with cocktails in our hands and healthy conversation about baseball, the boys, the competition, and whatever else we had in common. The siblings played in the pool and occasionally lured us away from the shady spots to throw a ball or play a game of Marco Polo.

Day 3: Sunday, August 5

Sunday might have been the first day I decided to go for a run with Tina Stephens, Bradley's mom. Even at 8:00 in the morning, it was 85 degrees. Tina and I run about the same speed, but she was training for a half marathon, I was not. The three mile run just about killed me. My mouth was so dry that my lips were stuck to my teeth. The heat was crippling. We ran a few more times in San Bernardino, each time the weather made it torturous.

It was a non-game day. Eric sent out a Huddle message saying we could take the boys for the entire day and bring them back for dinner.

There were a lot of Huddle messages back to Eric asking if it was ok to take the boys to the water park. His vague answer was subject to interpretation. I think it was something like, "Be careful, don't spend too much time in the sun and use good judgment." Ok, so some of us interpreted that as, it's ok to go to the waterpark, but keep the boys in the shade as much as possible and limit the amount of time at the park. The small group of families who ventured to the water park ensured no one got hurt, no one got sunburned and everyone had fun. And, if you can believe it, the water park had a bar. Bonus!

Day 4: Monday, August 6

Our game on Monday, August 6 wasn't until 8pm. So, Bailey and I went on a road trip to UCLA and Loyola Marymount. Kailyn and Cathy Paretti, Austin's Sister and Mother, went with us. Kailyn and Bailey were both seniors at Petaluma High looking forward to attending college in the fall of 2013. After about 2 hours of travel time, we arrived. Both campuses were lovely, and it was a nice break for us to get away from baseball. We arrived back in Colton with just enough time to change into our red gear and head to the game.

By now, the entire fan base was accustomed to arriving at least one hour before the game start time to support the boys as they came out of the dorm to head to the field for warm up. They would walk single file with their coaches through the crowd to the field. We all liked to be there to line their way, cheer them on, and give them hugs and high fives. Teddy was always there to have his hair rubbed for good luck! He knew his role and he played it well.

The rumor was that in the past, the Northern California, Southern California games were the most well attended. This concerned me a bit, because the crowd really does play a role in each game. The good news was the rivalry game was on a Monday night (not the weekend), so the Southern California crowd was big, but not overwhelming.

We defeated Southern California that evening. It was 98 degrees when the game was over at 10 pm. The boys went back into the dorms, changed, then came out to say goodnight to fans and parents.

Day 5: Tuesday, August 7

We had a record of 3-0 going into the Tuesday evening game. Eric had told us at the outset of the tournament if we had a winning record of 3-0, we would likely be in the semi-finals. We were very excited. On Tuesday, August 7, at the hotel pool, in the shady corner, with drinks in hand, the conversation of the day was about how nice it was the boys had made it to San Bernardino and were going to participate in the finals. Not one parent mentioned Williamsport, not one parent mentioned winning the championship in San Bernardino, but I know I was thinking about it. I know we were all secretly thinking about it.

The Nevada game that night was not pretty, we were ahead, then we got a little sloppy and Nevada scored a few. Thankfully, we finished the game with a win.

Back at the hotel that night, Jon Banister got us all laughing with one of his one liners, "This team is like a bunch of alcoholics, they don't even get started until the bottom of the fifth." Cracked us all up. He was right, the boys seemed to come alive late in the games which made most games very exciting.

Day 6: Wednesday, August 8

Wednesday was a non-game day, I think it was 108 degrees again. This time, when Eric sent out the Huddle to say we could take the boys, he "ok'ed" an official trip to the water park, and the entire group (I think there were 50 or so of us) headed there. Bob and Bailey skipped the water park and went on another college road trip to visit University San Diego and San Diego State University.

Everyone, including the coaches, enjoyed the water park (again). This time, the bar was not open (they missed out on some good business that day). I guess we should have called ahead?

Day 7: Thursday, August 9

The boys were busy all day. They were practicing and then hitting at the local batting cages. The batting cage staff opened up early for the boys to accommodate their schedule. After the batting cages, the boys watched the other teams play. At this point in the tournament, it was serious business. The players were hyper alert on the standings, who was playing well, who was pitching. They were watching everything and thinking about nothing but winning the next game.

By this time, our boys had made great friends with the Northwest team from Oregon. The dorms were arranged so that on one side there was a dorm for a team, in the middle was a bathroom and on the other side of the bathroom was another team. Oregon and Northern California shared a bathroom and became great friends. Oregon was competing for the Northwest Championship. Petaluma was competing for the West Championship, so the two teams would never face off unless they both went to Williamsport and the West faced the Northwest. Because the boys became such good friends and supported each other at the games, the parents also became friendly. We were calling each other by first names, and rooting each other on like the boys were teammates. The Petaluma boys, coaches and parents could not say enough words of praise about the Oregon players and parents.

Sometime earlier in the week, we had discovered Rico's Tacos. It was across the parking lot from the Hampton Inn pool. YUMMMM! The tacos were $1.60 (no joke), and they were amazing. We added a new activity to the pool tradition, eating Rico's tacos.

Back at the pool, while we were standing in the shady corner, with drinks in one hand, Rico's tacos in the other, Jon Banister told us a story from the batting cages. He was watching the boys hit and there was a father there with his young son maybe 9 years old. The father saw Bradley Smith and said "Hey, aren't you with the Northern California team?" Bradley answered "Yes."

The father said "I pick you guys to go all the way."

Bradley said "All the way where?" The father replied "All the way to Williamsport."

Bradley said "Oh." Standing in the pool, a group of us laughed until we cried. The phrase of the day was "All the way where?"

Day 8: Friday, August 10

Today was our daughter's 17th birthday. And, today was our son's semi-final game, two major milestones. One got media attention, the other did not get much attention at all. We talked to Bailey in the days leading up to her birthday and she assured us she was happy to spend her special day in San Bernardino. She said "I will have many more birthdays. Blake is having a moment of a lifetime." Have I already written how blessed Bob and I are? Bailey is that kind of person. The kind of person you always want to be your friend. The kind of person who understands issues and conflicts far beyond her years. We love her for that. But, Bob and I still felt guilty.

Some of the moms got out for a manicure and pedicure in the morning. I sent Bailey to get pampered on her birthday. She had her toe nails painted in a bright red in yet another vote of support for her brother.

We spent the afternoon in the lobby of the Hampton Inn with glitter, glue, poster board, markers and scissors making posters for the boys. Today was to be their first appearance on ESPN, and each parent or sibling made a custom sign for their player. What a royal mess we made in that lobby. Think red glitter on a dark colored rug. Think sticky glue all over at least 10 tables. It was interesting to watch each parent. Some spent hours on their signs. Some spent hours cutting out stars for everyone else. Some let the siblings make the signs. At the end, every boy was well represented and the lobby was a big, fat, sticky, glittery mess.

This is where I give special kudos to the staff of the Hampton Inn. Wow, they did not seem frazzled at all. They got out their sponges, their vacuum and some sticky rollers (like the kind you use to get lint off your clothes) and started the cleanup effort. When we offered to help, they smiled and turned us down. They had that place back to "normal" in an hour or so. But, the next morning while eating breakfast, I did see some stray red sparkles stuck in the carpet. Frankly, I think it added a bit of bling to the lobby.

As usual, we arrived an hour before the game to cheer on the boys as they left the dorm. This time, we were equipped with customized, sparkly, red signs. The Oregon boys were right in line with us cheering on the team as they walked to the field for warm up. When we arrived to our seats in the stands, we were greeted by the ESPN cameraman and an assistant. They explained how we were to engage with them. The assistant would write the on-deck batter's jersey number on a small white board. He would wave it in front of the crowd, at which time, we were to point to the right set of parents so the cameraman could film the right people when their son was at bat. Pretty non-technical, but it worked perfectly. When our kids were not at bat, the cameraman moved to the other team's bleacher area.

Unless you have had an ESPN camera in your face, you cannot understand the tension. First, your batter is on national TV, more than anything, you want your son to get a hit while at the plate. But, now, instead of cheering your heart out, making emotional facial contortions, and potentially whispering bad words under your breath, all you can do is sit there smiling. And, for the first time ever, it seemed like each time Blake was at bat was an eternity. The camera just kept staring until he was either safely on base, or back into the dugout. Serious parent stress out.

They won the game against Nevada. During the game, I received several texts from friends at home with pictures of me, Bob, Bailey and Blake on TV. This was our first real signal people back home in Petaluma were watching. Receiving the texts and pictures were very cool and somewhat alarming. I seriously need to sit up straight, stop slouching, and maybe smile a bit more. Yikes!

After the game, Eric told us we could take the boys for 1 hour to a quick dinner, but we had to have them back by 10pm. So much for a birthday celebration for Bailey with the group, we zipped off to the closest pizza parlor we could find, and the four of us talked about the game. Blake told Bailey "Happy Birthday" and that he was sorry she was spending her special day in San Bernardino. She smiled and assured him it is what she wanted to do. Bob and I were happy that we had at least one hour of precious time with the four of us. Then, we returned Blake at the field by 10 and went to the grocery store and bought cookies and candles to share with everyone in the hotel lobby and sing happy birthday to Bailey and Mereena. It was also Mereena, Dylan's mom's birthday. We got to the lobby and no one was there. Most of the rest of the team had all gone to a Mexican restaurant and were still there, waiting for their food. We went up to our room, lit a candle, and Bob and I sang Bailey the Happy Birthday song. She blew out the candle and made a wish. Super guilt!

Day 9: Saturday, August 11

This day was the beginning of a very difficult to describe, perpetual baseball stress. The kind of stress where your heart pounds on the inside, but you have to look and act like you are holding it together on the outside. I know my husband and I were experiencing it, but neither one of us talked about it.   I have very little recollection of what the heck we did during the day of Saturday, August 11. Most likely it involved standing in the shady deep end, with a drink in our hand, eating Rico's tacos, but I cannot tell you for sure because I was seriously stressed out. Again, no one spoke of Williamsport, no one spoke of what could be next, we just talked about the game at hand, the fact that we had played Hawaii before, who was going to pitch, and stuff like that. Nobody mentioned the word "win." Nobody.

At this point, the team was among the 52 best that played at eight regional tournaments in the United States and among the best of 79 teams in eight international regionals. Go Petaluma National Little League!

We headed to the game dressed in our traditional red, with our red, sparkly parent signs, an hour early to greet the boys. They did not seem anxious at all. They were ready to play, just like any other game.

The championship game for the West region started at 5pm. Much like the previous day, we assumed our seats, along with the ESPN cameraman and assistant and the boys did their thing.

Hawaii jumped out to a 2-0 lead in the first inning. Then, Logan Douglas tied the game with a two-run homer that drove in Porter Slate. Danny Marzo and Kempton Brandis singled and took advantage of some good base running which put the score at 3-2

Hawaii came back in the second to retake the lead at 4-3. Petaluma scored four runs in three hits, two walks and an error with some aggressive base running in the fourth inning.   Petaluma was up 7-4.

In the sixth, with two outs and runners at first and second, Hawaii hit a line drive to left field that got past Dylan Moore and rolled to the wall. The Hawaii base runners on first and second scored two runs on the error. But, Porter saw that the second runner failed to touch third base and appealed the play. Upon appeal, the third base umpire raised his hand formed it into the "you're out" gesture and the game was over. Great heads-up play by Porter!

It was real, the Petaluma National Little League team just won themselves a trip to Williamsport, Pennsylvania to represent the Western Region of the United States in the 66th annual Little League World Series.

Outbursts of emotions from players, fans and particularly Dads happened all over again. The tears were flowing. Have you ever hugged someone with so much sheer emotion that both of your bodies shake with excitement and joy? I have. We were all hugging, shaking and crying. From behind the fence above the dugout, just out of reach, we watched our sons hug, cry, laugh, scream and jump around in excitement. What did it feel like for them? What were they thinking? Did they ever let themselves think it could happen? I could not imagine what was inside their heads, but I could surely see their love of the game and their winning spirit. What a moment!!

After the boys were presented with the West Championship banner, they were hurried off to the press room where we were to join them for the parent meeting. Only a special few get to go to the parent meeting and today, we were part of that special few. I looked at Bob and whispered "How did we get here?" I did not expect an answer, and he did not offer one.

As we were walking off the field, we had to pass by the Hawaii fans and parents. Many of them had already walked out of the stadium to meet their players, but some lingered. There were some very kind words like "Great game! Go all the way!," and some not so kind words like "you did not deserve to win." My family walked quietly and humbly by to meet the winning team in the press room. I wondered how I would feel if I were not walking to the parent meeting.

In the meeting, we were met by the boys and got some very brief hugs. We were there for business, so we sat down and listened. The Petaluma National Team would go to the Little League World Series representing the

West region of the United States. And, as luck would have it, their new friends from Oregon, who had secured the Northwest Championship would be accompanying them. As I looked around, I thought how lucky it was for both of these teams, who had become so close, to be making the next step in this journey together. Very cool. The speaker, who had come to San Bernardino representing the Little League World Series, introduced himself and explained he was there to make sure the boys were transported to Williamsport safely, and the parents were informed. He clearly had given the presentation many times before, but he still exuded excitement for the boys and what was ahead of them. He told us in all of his years of experience, there have been countless people who bragged to him "I took part in the Little League World Series," but he went on to say this group of players could say that same thing only they could say it "honestly."

The parent meeting went on way too long. The basic information was disseminated, like how the boys would leave for Williamsport, Pennsylvania the next morning, their new team colors, when they would arrive, where they would stay, who would do their laundry, blah, blah, blah. The factor that kept the meeting going was the question and answer session. The boys and some parents started asking all kinds of nervous, somewhat unimportant questions. Questions like "What's the weather like?," "Who will be our roommates?" "Are the beds more comfortable?" "Will I be able to checkout my son?" All I wanted to do was get out of there, have time with my son, and relish in the final moments before he left with the team for the 66th annual Little League World Series.

As the dumb questions continued, I looked over at the giant window in the meeting room and saw a few of the Hawaii players looking in longingly, some with tears and puffy eyes. My heart ached for them. No one who took part in the San Bernardino event wanted to be on the outside looking in. In baseball, there is one winner and one loser. Thankfully, today, we came out on top.

Following the parent meeting, the plan was the boys would come to the Hampton Inn for a quick party, then back to the barracks before 10pm so they could pack and get ready for their trip to Williamsport early the next morning.

When we got back to the hotel lobby, family, friends and fans had set up a pizza party for the families and boys. The staff at the hotel put up a big sign honoring the West Champions, and the pizza, soda, cookies, wine, beer and water were plentiful. No one sat to eat. We all walked around, took a few bites, hugged each other and talked to our sons. It was such a proud evening for everyone there. The energy in the room was astounding. The boys learned their team colors would be yellow and green and from that point forward they were to be called the "West". In the lobby that night, it was like the wild, wild West!

The final morning in San Bernardino, we packed up our luggage said goodbye to the hotel staff and headed one last time to the field. We met Blake outside the dorm, gave him a bunch of big hugs, and spending money, made sure his phone was charged and kissed him goodbye. I said, "See you on the other side." He smiled a really confident 12 year old smile. Priceless.

A quote from the media on what Manager Eric Smith thought of the tournament win:

> "It's not that I didn't think they could do it, but so many things have to go right, and you have to play so many days in a row. It's amazing they were able to accomplish it. We never made our goal to go to the Little League World Series, but to be better baseball players and better students and carry ourselves well."

We came to find out sometime later that Eric Smith won a coach's award in San Bernardino. I am not sure what the award was, or how he was selected and honored. But, what I do know for sure was it was well deserved.

West Region Championship Results

Win: Petaluma National Little League (PNLL) 11, Hawaii 9

Win: Petaluma National Little League (PNLL) 2, Arizona 1

Win: Petaluma National Little League (PNLL) 3, Southern California 2

Win: Petaluma National Little League (PNLL) 10, Nevada 6

Win: Petaluma National Little League (PNLL) 10, Nevada 4

Win: Petaluma National Little League (PNLL) 7, Hawaii 5

5 - THE 66TH ANNUAL LITTLE LEAGUE WORLD SERIES – AUG 16-26

Getting to Williamsport

On Sunday, the boys were on their way to Pennsylvania, and the Buhrer family minus Blake was back home in Petaluma. It did not seem odd that Blake was not with us, rather it felt strange that we were not immediately following him. In a frenzied manner, we tried to find hotels in the Williamsport area with a block of rooms to house the parents of 13 kids. Apparently, the West was the last team trying to find hotel reservations. All the other teams had already secured their arrangements. Very quickly, each family gave up on trying to get a block of rooms and independently starting booking what we could find. For the first time on the journey, it was every family for themselves. We were resigned to being in different locations. We all just wanted to get there.

As a suggestion for the future, I think the Little League Organization should block 15 hotel rooms for each team's families well in advance of the win. Then, once the region wins occur, the parents should be offered the block of rooms. That way, there is not too much scrambling. But, I am not even sure to whom I should direct the suggestion.

On Sunday night, I finally reached Zack at the Genetti hotel's reservation desk. He said he had a room available, but we would have to prepay and during our stay, we would have to move rooms two times.

In desperation, I said "OK." After I committed to booking he said, "I have to take your number and call you back, I have Jeff O'Hanlan, James' father, on the other line, and I am booking a room for him."

I said to Zack "Ok, but tell Jeff to hurry it up." Zack called me back shortly, and we secured a prepaid hotel room at a ridiculously high rate for Wednesday through Sunday night. Bob and I had agreed we would book and prepay only for the first 5 nights, if the boys lost early, we would head back home. If they won, we would have to negotiate a new hotel room, or spend the night on some other family's hotel floor.

We had a discussion with Bailey about whether or not she would come with us to Williamsport. We collectively decided she would stay home, go on an unplanned camping trip (as a sort of substitute to the one we had to cancel) with her friends, and start her high school senior year with the support of family friends at home. We agreed if the team made it into the final weekend, we would fly her out for the games. This was a tough decision. She was torn, because she wanted so much to continue to support her brother, but also wanted to spend time with her friends who were preparing to leave for college. It was a tough decision for Bob and I, too, because we had never left Bailey behind. She was 17, she was ready to make the tough decision and ready to be independent in her own home. Were we ready to let go? We had to be. We booked two one way flights to Pittsburg, Pennsylvania. We left the return flight open, just in case. We were lucky to get the flight; there were very few seats left at a ridiculously high ticket price. On the flight, we both had middle seats a few aisles away from each other. Whatever, we just needed to get there!

We contacted Jeff and Jackie O'Hanlan, James' parents, and agreed to share the rental of a single car since we were on the same flight, and both had reservations at the Genetti Hotel in Williamsport.

Blake had been in contact with us regularly since he arrived in Williamsport. He usually called his Dad in the evenings just before or after dinner. He did not chat long, but he gave us some insight into the flurry of excitement swirling thousands of miles away. He told us he had met the other teams, and they were all very nice. He said they received their uniforms and cleats. He was so thrilled the cleats were stamped prominently with the words "Little League World Series." Later we found out some of the Uganda players had arrived without shoes and dilapidated equipment. Imagine the excitement those kids had when they tried on a pair of specialty cleats. It must have been like Christmas morning!

Back in San Bernardino, there was a small Easton gear booth. One day, while we were walking around with Blake, we stopped to admire the unreleased 2013 Easton bats. Blake practically drooled at the glistening new stick. The young man working the booth told us each boy on the teams who made it to Williamsport would receive one of the coveted bats. We left he booth thinking those were gonna be some lucky kids! Who knew they would be from Petaluma?

Blake was giddy when he told us he received his new, 2013 Easton bat. To select a bat, one by one, the players went into a batting cage, and practiced. They were assessed on how they performed, then given the bat that worked best for them individually. Blake could hardly contain himself enough to explain the process to us over the phone. For him, the bottom line was he was at the Little League World Series. He had a new uniform, new cleats and a new Easton bat. Being on the phone with his curious parents seemed such a nuisance.

Huddle Messages

I have included direct quotes from the team's Huddle messages. Starting in San Bernardino, this is the way Manager, Eric Smith, communicated with the thirteen families and the way we mass messaged each other. We waited anxiously for every message. The Huddle excerpts are sometimes cryptic, and often funny, and a perfect representation of the chaotic nature of the communications between parents and coaches at the Little League World Series. The name in parenthesis at the end of each Huddle message is the "nickname" a parent selected when they signed on as a Huddle member. All time stamps on the Huddle messages are in EST unless otherwise noted.

From Williamsport

> 9:37am: Kids are getting sick. I want to get preventative medicine. Does anyone have concerns about Zicam? If so, text me directly. Does not need to be huddled (EricSmith)
>
> Go for anything reasonable to help (Drew4Reds)

11:07am: all awake now. Looking good (EricSmith)

From Petaluma

Is anyone leaving 2day? Please text me on my phone if u r. thank you. (Moma-cat)

9:17am (PST): Don't forget dine and donate tonight at Beyond the Glory. It includes take out too as I know we are all busy packing. Please tell everyone you know! (UCLAHeather)

3:22pm (PST) do we have 2 pay to get into games (Moma-cat)

No (drew4Reds)

News crews are going to be at Beyond the Glory at 5pm to interview parents, etc. If you can get there by then, please do! Spread the word please (UCLAHeather)

Day 1: Wednesday, August 15

The O'Hanlans and Bob and I arrived very early at the San Francisco airport. Our flight was on Virgin Airlines. We were waiting in the long line to check in our luggage, when someone called out Bob's name. He left the line to speak with a lovely young woman who was heading up the "premier" check in line. He motioned to us to move to the premier line. We wheeled our luggage over and were introduced to a woman wearing a Virgin Airline shirt, Kayla, Bob's cousin's daughter. Bob and I had not seen her since she was a child. She graciously allowed us to check in with the premier passengers (there were not any in line at the time). During the check in process, she was able to find us seats next to each other on the flight. What luck reconnecting with Kayla that day!

The flight was perfectly uneventful. When we landed, we found our rental car and the Buhrers and O'Hanlans were off on a lovely drive from Philadelphia to Williamsport. The landscape was so lush and green. When we were just outside of Williamsport, the sky decided to show us why all the foliage was so beautiful. We were caught in the most unexpected, intense downpour of rain for about 15 minutes. Ok, now we got it. Pennsylvania has green plants in the summer because it has crazy, unpredictable rain storms that soak the earth and everything else! So not like California weather. We were hoping to experience an electrical storm, but no luck.

<u>Huddle Messages</u>

From Williamsport

6:59pm: What's the scoop on the parade? Time and start and finish? (UCLAHeather)

Drew said it started at 6:00. Not sure when it ends. Not sure if rain affected it (Drewsdad)

We haven't even boarded our float yet. It is raining hard at the moment (trev49)

Is parade over? A block away, can't park near hotel (Gagomama)

It was early evening when we finally arrived into Williamsport proper. We had some trouble getting to our hotel because the 66th annual Little League parade was underway, and many of the streets surrounding the hotel were blocked. We finally gave up, parked on a side street and walked to the parade. When we reached the parade, we were told we had just missed the Petaluma team. Darn! We progressed to the hotel desk and checked in.

Bob was already in the room with our luggage when I entered. He met me at the door and said, "You are not going to like this." I said, "I am sure it is fine, I am just happy I have a place to sleep."

What a liar I am. That room was straight out of a horror movie. The floor was filthy and spotted with cigarette burns. The bed linens were dingy and balled, the wall paper was hanging from the corners and brown with age. The bathroom was ghastly. The toilet did not have a bowl under it. It had a rusty old "kick flush" system attached to the wall. The shower was dark, small and putrid. Under the sink, I found the rusty blow dryer, accompanied by mouse droppings. How was I going to make it through 5 days (or longer) in this room? After I texted Blake to tell him we had arrived, I turned out the lights and went to bed. At least in the dark, I could pretend the hotel was acceptable.

From Williamsport

9:30pm: Kids are in bed and had a snack (EricSmith)

11:00pm: parent meeting at Lamade Stadium tomorrow (NicoleM)

What time? (UCLAHeather)

9:30 (NicoleM)

Day 2: Thursday, August 16

The Day

Think about flying to a place you had never thought about visiting, with tentative hotel arrangements, no return flight, a tentative schedule for each day, and little or nothing to do but wait in anticipation. That is how each day started in Williamsport. I was forced to let go of the organized standards of my "ordinary life" and learn to be ok with whatever happened. The perpetual baseball stress that started in San Bernardino continued. I was fighting to hold it together. I suspected many of the parents felt the same.

The next morning, Bob said he had made friends with Kathy at the hotel's front desk and she was going to move our room that day. I was a little apprehensive. Our room was beyond acceptable, but what if she moved us to another room that was the same or worse? Was it possible? I spoke with her and she explained the room we were staying in was usually reserved by pipe workers in the area. They rent the rooms for months at a time at a very low rate. The room where she was moving us was part of the hotel nightly rental block of rooms. The new room, 420, was a huge improvement. Kathy had even upgraded us (for a few more dollars) to a suite. I could have kissed her! Instead, Bob gave her his coveted Little League San Bernardino hat. Small price to pay for the work she did for us. Kathy was our hero!

We were scheduled to be at the field at 9:00 am for a parent meeting. We drove from the Genetti hotel to the field in under 10 minutes. Bonus. I was grateful the hotel was so close to the field. We parked as directed by the volunteers that were assisting the newbies (like us) to the right areas. When we left the car, I made the decision to leave behind my jacket and my camera since I did not want to tote them around..

About half way to the field, I promptly turned around and went back to the car to get my camera. What was I thinking? There were photo opportunities everywhere. What a beautiful facility. On the way to Volunteer Stadium, on the right hand side of the walkway was a giant "Welcome to the Little League World Series" meticulously crafted in dark green bushes. Wow.

We were entering the park from below Volunteer Stadium and were required to pass through metal detectors and have our bags searched. At that point, it occurred to me that this event had international attention, and there would likely be a lot of security in place. Hmm. Should I be concerned? I hoped not.

Volunteer stadium is the smaller of the two on the campus, and where most of the international teams would play. As we walked past the stadium I was in awe. It was lovely. San Bernardino's field was like a little league field on steroids, Volunteer Stadium was like a big league field scaled down. Amazing.

Because I had gone back to get my camera, I was late when I finally entered Lamade Stadium. So, I hurried to the seat Bob had saved me. Once I settled, I took a moment and looked around. This stadium was even more spectacular. The field was perfectly groomed. There were announcer and camera booths, giant lights, and sunken dugouts. Now this was just like the big leagues. Holy cow. We were in Lamade Stadium, at a parent meeting because our son, Blake, was going to play in the 2012 Little League World Series. Pinch me!

Parent meeting number 2 was well organized and fairly quick compared to parent meeting number 1 in San Bernardino. The most noteworthy information was that each team would receive 42 lanyards that identified the team parents and family and entitled the wearers to preferred seating.

Nicole Marzo, Danny's mom, had the task of dolling out the 42 lanyards. As the week progressed and family and friends came and went, the lanyard allocations proved to be very challenging. Nicole handled it well, there were times she gave away her own children's lanyards to other families and had her children sit among the non-family crowd. It is a good thing I was not in charge of handing out the lanyards, because closer to the end of the week when the demand for the lanyards exceeded supply, and the pressure to hand them out to the right beggar increased, I may have strangled myself. I considered the necklace a badge of honor that connected me to a beloved player

While we were sitting at the parent meeting one smart parent snuck away and returned wearing a very bright West team jersey. He slithered back into his seat with a sly smile. Aha, he was smart getting to the gift shop before all the parents were dismissed.

Bob and I caught on. Just as the parent meeting was ending, and they were passing out the lanyards, Bob and I made a frantic beeline to the gift shop just outside of Lamade Stadium. There was a person at the entry door of the gift shop whose sole responsibility was to watch the exit door, count the number of people that left, then open the entry door and allow that same number of people to enter. We were about 10 people deep in the line to get in. The color assigned to the West was, as I called it, screaming yellow. The screaming yellow West section was located in the far back left corner. We headed there with our list which included jerseys, sweatshirts and hats for the family, t-shirts and hats for friends and pins. In the course of the next 20 minutes, we had purchased $487 worth of gear, and we knew we would be back to buy more if the boys played well. When we exited the gift shop, the line to get in was over 50 people deep. As the week went on the line fluctuated between 50-100 people waiting to spend money on Little League logo wear.

Before opening ceremonies, we put on our screaming yellow West jerseys and hats and explored the facility. We found the Grove, where the boys were staying, and the parent tent. The parent tent is just inside the Grove and is the place where players go to spend time with their family after games, away from the crowds and media. The players would come and go from the Grove onto the general property, but could not leave the campus without permission from their team manager. So, we could see Blake in the Grove parent tent, or on the fields when he had time to come out and watch other games or interact with the fans. Bob and I never had the opportunity to tour the Grove (other than the parent tent). I think they might have offered parent tours in the days before we arrived.

After many of our team parents visited the gift shop, about 40 of us headed to the opening ceremonies at Volunteer stadium. It was not possible to miss the West crowd, we looked like a giant yellow amoeba moving to our seats. The ceremony started and the West team was the first to be introduced. They marched on the field with their Uncles (the parent volunteers assigned to the team) and coaches. Each player held onto a string with a yellow balloon attached. One by one, each team was announced as they paraded onto the field. All sixteen teams took their place around the outside of the bases facing in toward the pitching mound. With each team introduction, the field became more colorful and crowded. Once all of the teams were on the field, it was a Walt Disney vision. So much color, so much energy from all the players and coaches. On prompt, all of the boys released their balloons just as they had done at the ceremony in San Bernardino. The balloons entwined. It was 80 degrees outside, but I got the chills.

The remainder of the opening ceremonies was a series of welcome messages and speeches. Then, each team received a box filled with one Little League medal for each player and coach (think Olympic Gold medal). Then, the teams were dismissed in an organized way accompanied by a giant round of applause to do what they do best, play baseball.

Huddle Messages

From Williamsport

11:11am: Someone filming opening ceremonies? (Drew4Reds)

Hello??? (Drew4Reds)

We took still pics. Sonny took some video (Gagomama)

Since we arrived in Williamsport, we had yet to talk to or hug Blake, but he knew we were there because we had a text exchange with him and we locked eyes and waved at opening ceremony.. He was prepping for game. We learned that some of the boys were not feeling well. Bob and I were hoping they could pull it together to make a good showing at game number one.

<u>Huddle Messages</u>

From Williamsport

12:40am: I have team VIP passes. Find me at the stadium to get yours (NicoleM)

The Game

<u>Huddle Messages</u>

From Williamsport

1:59pm: Let's go Petaluma!!! Let's Go West!!! (Ricardo)

From Petaluma

I am still in Petaluma representing for all of us at the theaters!!! Cheer for me everyone!!! (RachelBrandis)

The first game was scheduled for 3:10 against the New England team from Connecticut. I figured out that the game started at 3:10 because it was filmed live, and the first 10 minutes were introduction footage, commercials, etc. We arrived at 1:30 hoping we might see the boys or at least say "Hi" to them during warm ups. It was hot and muggy, but not hellish like San Bernardino.

When Bob and I arrived in the parent section, we selected two seats next to the aisle. Bob is a "pacer," when the game gets intense, he has a hard time staying in his seat, so he paces around. He wanted to take the end seats so if he needed to walk around, he would not disturb the entire row of people on his way out or in. What we did not realize when we took the end seats was the aisle to the side of us was a main corridor for the ESPN camera crew. Hmm. Maybe not the best seat selection. But, once we had all sat down, and we started winning, we were not moving. These were our lucky seats for the tournament. No one was going to mess with the mojo.

At the start of each game Dugout (the Little League mascot) would come out and do a dance on the field with the teams. I am not sure if that was televised, but it was cute and I think it helped the boys relax a little right before the start of the game.

Apparently Connecticut, the team representing the New England region, had been undefeated in their battle to win their region. Would this be a tough game? Bradley Smith our starting pitcher, came out, pitched four strong innings, giving up two runs (one earned) and striking out seven batters.

The New England team stayed in the hunt the entire game. I think our boys had a bit of the first game jitters, but they still executed well. At one point, they had a sloppy defensive play on a delayed double steal. I was surprised because I have seen them execute that play many times effectively.

Andrew White, the team's usual closer, came in to relieve Bradley in the 5th inning and had a rough start. His first Little League World Series pitch hit the Connecticut batter in the face. When the pitch hit the batter, the grandstands went quiet. We waited. The West boys on the field took a knee. There was a lot of blood. Eventually, the batter was removed from the field, and we later learned the pitch had hit his wrist before hitting his mouth taking some of the impact, but he received two stiches in his mouth. He was cleared to play in his next game (with some enhanced protective gear). Phew. Andrew recovered from the bad pitch, to strike out two New England players, ending the fifth. I was amazed at Andrew's mental ability to recover and pitch well after the batter injury. Later, Andrew personally apologized to the injured player.

In the top of the sixth, Danny Marzo hit a homerun and put the score at 6-4. That was the final score of the game. Our first win at the 66th Little League World Series! We came to play, we played to win. The 42 lanyards were swinging up and down on 13 families as we hugged each other hard.

Later, we learned from the press that during the game, the West pitchers ended every inning with a strike out. Very nice.

Blake told me that during the game, one of his coaches pointed out to the players that the Oregon boys were there cheering them on. It meant a lot to the Petaluma team that their Oregon buddies were there for support.

Huddle Messages

From Williamsport

> 5:11pm: Meet the boys in the big white tent at the top of the hill (BeckySmith)

After the game, we immediately headed for the parent tent so we could celebrate the win with our boys. We climbed the 60 (or so steps) from Lamade Stadium to the Grove and waited patiently with our parent lanyards dangling around our necks. We waited for at least 20 minutes before someone told us the boys had to change out of their uniforms and eat before they would join us in the tent. We were used to waiting by now, so we waited some more. The parents of the New England team were also waiting. I wondered what would happen next. Would both teams go into the one parent tent? How would that work out? What I came to figure out as the week went on, was the winning team got to pick whether they met the boys in the tent or outside of the Grove. Tonight, we met the boys in the tent, the Connecticut parents met their kids outside of the Grove. I am not sure the tent was the best choice, it was full of irritating little gnats.

The boys were happy they had a win, but some of them were clearly still not feeling well. We made the visit quick so the team could get back to their dorms and get a good night of rest. Blake told us the dorms were much better than San Bernardino, assured us that he was turning in his clothes to be laundered and said he was having a lot of fun meeting the other boys. He was not feeling sick. As any good mother would do, I told him to keep washing his hands. Then, I waved my hands to clear away the gnats and gave him a hug good night.

From Williamsport

> 8:02pm: A company would like to make bobble heads of our boys
> from the newspaper pics. Please contact me tonight if you have an
> issue with this (BeckySmith)

We returned to the hotel Genetti's bar (which I nicknamed the Genetti
Cave because of its dark wood work and sunken entrance). I celebrated our
first win with a glass of mediocre red wine, Bob had a beer. Others enjoyed
mixed drinks. The celebration conversation that night was in honor of
making it to Williamsport, and winning one game. I remember one parent
said, "Now whatever happens is just icing." I don't think he really meant it,
but what else could he say? The unspoken truth was we did not travel
2,000 miles for one win.

Day 3: Friday, August 17

The Day

Huddle Messages

From Williamsport

> 9:14am: 10 hitting, 12:30 lunch, 2:00 museum. If anyone wants
> their kid after that I need to know before lunch (EricSmith)
>
> I also need to know if they will miss 5:30 dinner (EricSmith)
>
> Last note, Oregon plays at 8:00. The boys will want to see that
> (EricSmith)

Friday was a non-game day. Both Bob and I worked our jobs remotely
from our hotel room. It was not optimal, but we made it work. The room
had one desk that appeared to be a replica of an old roll top desk. It was
small, with an uncomfortable chair. I settled there to work. The sharp edge
of the desk dug into my right wrist as I used the computer mouse triggering

a carpel tunnel pain. Bob sat himself at a small round bed side table where he plugged in his computer. He pulled up a lounging chair to work, and I am sure he was just as uncomfortable. Neither of us complained.

Huddle Messages

From Williamsport

> 11:20am: Sonny – the store has visors. Navy blue with green piping (UCLA Heather)
>
> Do they say West? (Gagomama)
>
> No, little league world series (UCLAHeather)
>
> 12:56pm: My brother is looking to fly out tomorrow. Any suggestions on a place to stay for him and cost? (trev49)
>
> Author Note: Nobody responded to the huddle from Trevor. None of us were willing to take on finding a room for his brother. It was a battle we had already fought.

Later in the day, we returned to the field to buy even more West logo wear and to spend some time with Blake. This time, we parked at the Day's Inn which was at the top of the campus and closer to the field. There was a sign in the parking lot that said "Parking $5, pay inside." We did not walk inside, we did not pay $5. We just wanted to get to the field.

We crossed the busy street and entered from the Lamade Stadium side through security. The volunteer at the security confiscated my 2 oz. hand sanitizer. Really? Hand sanitizer? Whatever. We called Blake and he was already out of the Grove watching one of the games, so we headed to meet him. On the way, we stopped at the gift shop, because the line was not too long and dropped another $85 on more logo wear. At that time, we saw the sign that said they were sold out of MEA products. MEA was the Middle East, Africa team being represented by Uganda. What a group of boys and what a coach! There was so much media around that team their logo wear was completely sold out on day two of the series. Good for them!

Everyone was wearing their color – red.

Throughout the week, ESPN ran a story on the Uganda team. The story was riveting and heart wrenching. It described the team's overwhelming drive to get from their poverty stricken homes to the Little League World Series. Each time I watched the story, I teared up. Our journey was difficult, but theirs was historic. Never had a team from Africa participated in the event. Until now.

Huddle Messages

From Williamsport

1:55pm: We have to go into the museum all together. Anybody else coming? Walking in in a couple minutes? (UCLAHeather)

2:38pm: Mexico & Canada tied 8-8 after 2 (BeckySmith)

Earlier in the day, the team had done some ESPN interviews, and some hitting in the batting cages, visited the Little League Museum and the original Little League playing field. When we caught up with Blake, he was hanging out with Kempton Brandis at Volunteer stadium watching the Latin America (Panama) versus MEA (Uganda) game. When he and Kempton left their seats to come and greet us, we had a few minutes to chat, then, they were slowly surrounded by fans asking for autographs and pictures. It was kind of like watching ants that found a piece of candy. First, one fan checked them out, a few more would come around, then, there was a swarm trying to get to the center where the boys stood ready with Sharpie pens. Bob and I watched in wonder. Our 12 year old was signing autographs. So weird!

Huddle Messages

From Williamsport

5:15pm: Anyone interested in joining me for a pedicure tomorrow morning? (Drewsmom)

Sue at Petaluma Junior High will email 7th grade schedules this afternoon and 8th grade on Tuesday (BeckySmith)

8:32pm: Any spots for the Paretti clan in the Oregon section? We'd love to support (Cath4par)

How many seats are there? The Whites are stuck by the left field foul pole (Drewsdad)

Day 4: Saturday, August 18

The Day

<u>Huddle Messages</u>

From Williamsport

8:35am: Kids have batting practice at 10:00. We will try and do a short practice after or at 1:00 if field not available at 11:00 (EricSmith)

Kids may leave with you today after practice, but I need to know by lunch if they won't be here for dinner (EricSmith)

Lastly, I would tell you the boys haven't had a lot of time mixing with other teams because of tiredness/sickness early in the week. So don't be surprised if some kids ask to stay and take in this experience. (EricSmith)

For those who are going to run this morning, can you be in the lobby around 9:15? (BeckySmith)

You guys run without me this morning (trev49)

Saturday was another day off for the boys, no game. Again they spent the day with the media and at practice. Most parents stopped asking Eric if we could take the boys off the campus. In reality, they did not want to leave. They had everything they wanted and needed, new friends, fans, and a day full of baseball games to watch. Bob and I encouraged Blake to enjoy every moment, make new friends, and take it all in. I think he was doing just that.

I believe Saturday was the first and last time four of the moms, including me, went for a run. The good news was the weather was much more pleasant than San Bernardino, the bad news for me was two of the runners ran at a faster pace, and we got lost on the run which made it about a 6 mile escapade. Everyone was running and talking, I was just panting and trying to unstick my upper lip from my teeth. Water, I needed water! Someone please find me water.

We went to the field later Saturday to visit with Blake. A bit of the same as Friday. He was watching a game with his team mates. Then, he was signing autographs. I think he was getting used to these daily rituals. I was still in awe.

Huddle Messages

From Williamsport

6:01pm: Do we know what side Oregon is on tonight? (Drewsdad)

Home side. Stadium almost full now (BeckySmith)

Day 5: Sunday, August 19

The Day

Bob and I started having contingency plan conversations around what to do for our return flight. Of course we had these conversations in the privacy of our hotel room because it involved discussing options if the team won or lost. We never spoke "what if we lose" in public. That was just plain wrong.

We knew if the team continued to win, we would continue to stay. So, if they won Sunday's game, we were going to need to request an extension on our hotel room. If we lost Sunday's game, but won Monday's game, we would still need an extension. If we lost both Sunday's and Monday's games, we would need to leave on Tuesday. These discussions were stressful and plagued with "what if." At this point we just asked Kathy, at the front desk of the Genetti, to extend our hotel stay through Tuesday. We crossed our fingers that the winning would continue. We did not make a return flight commitment yet.

The Game

The game on Sunday was scheduled for 2 pm against the Southeast team from Goodlettsville, Tennessee

In the fourth inning, Kempton Brandis hit a homerun, and in the Fifth, Porter cracked one out too. The game was tied at 5-5 heading into the sixth, but Tennessee scored 4 runs making it 9-5 as the game headed into the bottom of the sixth inning. We attempted to execute a two out rally, but the game ended with a score of 9-6 in Tennessee's favor.

We climbed the 80 or so stairs to wait for the boys to change out of their uniforms and meet us at the parent tent (I know it was more like 60 stairs, but after a loss, it seemed like a very long haul). When I got to the top of the steps a pre-teen girl and her mother were waiting. The mother said, "Are you Porter's mom?"

I said, "No, but she will be here shortly. Can I help you?" The mother explained that her daughter had recovered Porter's homerun ball and wanted him to sign it.

"Oh" I said. I did my best to educate her on the homerun ball tradition. In Little League, if you recover a homerun ball you return it to the player for their collection. I went on to share this would be a special ball for Porter since it was a homerun at the Little League World Series.

I said, "Perhaps you can get Porter's autograph on your shirt and give him the ball." The daughter gripped the ball, smiled, and said, "I already have his autograph on my shirt."

She turned to show me the signatures of all the boys on the back of her screaming yellow West shirt. This was not my battle to fight. I told her I would send over Porter's mother when she arrived.

Heather, Porter's mom, appeared at the top of the stairs, I told her about the conversation with the mother and daughter. She was excited that someone had recovered Porter's homerun ball, and set off to talk to the pair to get the ball back for Porter's collection. It went bad fast. Porter did not get the homerun ball, and the pre-teen girl did not get his autograph on it either. Too bad. I wondered if that mother and daughter had any idea of the odds of any 12 year old playing in the World Series, and the intense emotion that is tied to hitting a homerun. I knew the answer was "nope."

The Tennessee parents waited at the top of the stairs, too. This time, the Tennessee team went into the tent with their boys (and the irritating gnats), and our boys exited the Grove to meet us. The boys were not down. There were no tears. In fact, I think they might have been ok with the loss. It meant they got to play more games because we dropped to the loser's bracket. Go Petaluma. Go West. Never give up.

Back at the Genetti Cave the conversation was around the statistics of coming from the loser bracket. The good news was teams do advance to win Little League baseball titles from the loser's bracket, including two of the past three champions – Huntington Beach in 2011, and Chula Vista in 2009. It was not out of reach.

By this time, we had been away from home for more than 12 days. I was seriously in need of some decent red wine. Please. I think this was the night we found the sports bar called "The Brickyard." It had 6 big screen televisions waiting for our crowd, and the staff willingly ran the Little League games for us to watch. Even more important, they had some drinkable red wine. Phew, out of the Genetti Cave for a while.

Bob and I secretly booked a flight home for Tuesday. If we lost the game on Monday, we wanted to get home, sleep in our own beds and eat food from our own refrigerator. By this time, I had figured out if we booked the flight and cancelled within 24 hours, there was no cancellation fee. So, I booked just late enough into the night, so by the end of the game tomorrow, if we won, I could cancel without any penalty. We had this down to a science.

Day 6: Monday, August 20

The Day

We checked in back home every day with Bailey with at least one phone call and lots of text messages. She had just returned from a short, impromptu camping trip with her friends who were getting ready to leave for college. We were happy she had a chance to do a little camping, but were feeling guilty that we had left her behind. She was scheduled to start school in two days. If we lost today, we could make it home in time to support her on her first day of her senior year.

<u>Huddle Messages</u>

From Williamsport

12:28pm: Do we know yet if we are home or visitors? (Drewsdad)

We are home. Tarp on field now (EricSmith)

1:47pm: Is any family member flying out 2morrow/ Emily's mom needs ride 2 airport (Moma-cat)

2:32pm: Think we will have a rain delay? (BobBuhrer)

3:15pm: Team just walked down from Grove. Game on their field in 4th inning. 17-1. (UCLAHeather)

The Game

<u>Huddle Messages</u>

From Williamsport

4:03pm: Let's GO Petaluma!!! (Ricardo)

Let's GO West!!! (Ricardo)

It's about time. Cutting it close Ricardo (Drewsdad)

Today's game was at 4 pm against the Mid Atlantic team from New Jersey. By now, the boys knew the routine. They danced with Dugout before the start of the game, and then came out to win.

This game was a true effort by the entire team. It was Blake, who got the team's rally started with a leadoff single past the second baseman in the bottom of the fourth. Petaluma was down 2-0 at that point. Danny Marzo followed Blake's hit with a single, bringing Bradley Smith to the plate. Bradley surprised New Jersey by laying down a perfect bunt and beating it out to first base. Logan Douglas, who was pinch-running for Blake, scored when an overthrow occurred at first.

Two batters later, shortstop, Hance Smith, knocked in two runs on a base hit between shortstop and third base, with Bradley Smith barely beating the relay throw.

1. After Bradley pitched, Logan Douglas came in as a relief and struck out four in 2 1/3 innings.

The team held a 4-2 lead at the start of the sixth inning. The, New Jersey team tied up the game at 4-4. Twice, the New Jersey team had a runner at third base, but could not score.

Finally, Danny Marzo put a fork in it with a walk off homerun at the bottom of the sixth.

As we had grown accustomed to doing, after the game, we climbed the now 100 steps (I swear the steps were multiplying) to the parent tent and waited to hug and congratulate Blake.

Back at the Genetti Cave, Bob went to have a beer, I ran upstairs to our room and cancelled our flight in the 24 hour no-penalty window. We would not make it home in time to see Bailey off to her first day as a senior in high school. Bob and I were happy, and full of guilt.

Huddle Messages

From Williamsport

9:05pm: We just got big table again at Brickyard. Same place as last night. They are happy to have us back! They serve food until 11. (UCLA Heather)

Day 7: Tuesday, August 21

The Day

<u>Huddle Messages</u>

From Williamsport

9:57am Boys are still sleeping. Oregon plays Uganda at 1:00. (EricSmith)

Rest is good. What time is lunch? (Ricardo)

Lunch scheduled for noon (EricSmith)

Do we know yet if we are home or visitors tonight? (Drewsdad)

That was the other thing – we are home (EricSmith)

Nice (Drewsdad)

11:32am: Boys are awake. Going to lunch in 15 minutes (EricSmith)

12:22pm: writer Kevin has four seats at Franco's at 5pm tonight for PNLLers. Let me know if anyone is interested. (Ricardo)

3:31pm: Cara from KTVU wants pictures from during and after game to put on the website. You can forward to me or Trevor (EricSmith)

5:19pm: FYI free massages for parents at Honda booth area (cath4par)

6:23pm: Let's Go Petaluma!!! (Ricardo)

Let's Go West!!! (Ricardo)

We had an entire day to ourselves in Williamsport. Our game was not until 8 pm at night. As I remember it, I started off the day by getting coffee downstairs in the Genetti and bringing back a warm cup for Bob. Then, I think I focused on laundry. The laundry room at the Genetti had two washing machines and three dryers. And, it was always busy. I met some very nice women there including parents from Texas and Tennessee. We mostly talked about laundry and not baseball. It seemed to be the most appropriate thing to do in the confined space while we waited for the wash and dryer cycles to finish. I wondered if they had been away from their homes for as long as we had. I wondered if they were yearning for their own beds and a good bottle of red wine. Forget it. I knew the answer, we were in this together. We each wanted to stay as long as necessary, but no longer than that. We were here for our sons. We would endure and embrace it all until the journey ended. Anyone have some quarters I can buy?

That afternoon, with Jeff and Jackie O'Hanlon, we took the advice of the hotel front desk staff and drove one hour to Penn's Cave. It is self-described as America's only all-water cavern and wild life park.

On the way to the caverns, we saw some Amish farms and some Amish people tending to their fields. Check that off my list, I have now seen the Amish (not just on television). The cavern tour via boat was interesting. There were two good things about the trip. First, the adventure killed 3 hours of our day while we waited for our next game time. Second, the cave was 55 degrees. It was the first time in 20 days where I wished I had a sweater. It felt like our Northern California evenings, cool and refreshing. The four of us noted the boys would have liked the trip through the cavern.

Again, before the game, I secretly booked another return flight home. If we won tonight, I would just cancel again.

The Game

Back at the Genetti Cave, we had a pre-game cocktail, for me it was a pre-game glass of mediocre wine. The parent conversation for pre-game was about our pitching challenges. Our two starting pitchers were not eligible based on the number of pitches they had thrown in previous games. Because we had dropped into the loser bracket we had more games to play, and pitching was beginning to be a challenge. The starting pitcher today would be Quinton Gago. Quinton had good pitching experience, but was not normally a starter.

Huddle Messages

From Williamsport

6:23pm: Let's Go Petaluma!!! (Ricardo)

Let's Go West!!! (Ricardo)

The game on Tuesday was at 8pm against the New England team from Connecticut, the same team we had defeated in our first game. Quinton came out strong. He ended up striking out seven, and allowing only two hits. At one point, he retired 11 consecutive Connecticut batters, including perfect innings in the third, fourth and fifth. Go Quinton. Andrew White came in later in the game to close.

Fairfield was desperate for a win. If they lost, they were out of the series. Cole Tomei had an amazing defensive play in the second inning as he charged a bunt, wheeled around and threw to third where Hance tagged the bag and threw to first for an outstanding double play.

Hance Smith hit his first homerun of the series. After the fourth inning, the score was at 4-0. In the fifth, Andrew White and Quinton both hit doubles and scored another run. The final score of the game was 5-0. The New England team from Fairfield, Connecticut was eliminated.

We climbed the 200 steps to the parent tent. When the team came out, after we gave our hugs and kudos to Blake, we chatted with Eric. We complimented him on the choice to start Quinton as the pitcher. He laughed and said, "I am not sure it was a good thing. I think he embarrassed me. Now everyone is going to ask why I had not started him before. I guess I will just say he was our secret weapon." Bob and I and the other parents heard his comment laughed. It was good to see Eric still had a sense of humor after the 20 or so days he had been sequestered with a bunch of 12 and 13 year old boys.

It was 10:30 pm before we got back to the hotel. I promptly went up to our room and cancelled our return flight home (again). The Fairfield fans and parents had already populated the Genetti Cave. To be gracious to the Connecticut team, we took our after game party over to the Brickyard, the sports bar we had discovered two blocks from our hotel. Good news for me, I celebrated with an acceptable glass of red wine (or maybe two).

Later that night, when we returned to the Genetti Cave, the Connecticut folks were still in the bar, and one Petaluma parent made a social blunder. He charged into the Cave, after having a few drinks at the Brickyard, and started to chant "Pet-a-luma." The Petaluma folks froze. We did not join in on the chant. The New England parents and fans stopped and stared. Awkward! Jackie, quickly shut down the social blunder and reminded everyone that we are all friends in the bar and we are not celebrating wins or losses, but instead celebrating a trip to the Little League World Series. Way to go Jackie. Phew.

Day 8: Wednesday, August 22

The Day

Wednesday, August 22 was the first day of seventh grade for Blake, he and twelve other boys would not be there. It was also the first day of school for Bailey, she attended with the remote support of her parents 2,000 miles away.

<u>Huddle Messages</u>

From Williamsport

11:06am: Parents are welcome at the original field tour. Please let me know. (EricSmith)

Also if you are taking your kid for dinner, you will need to follow bus back and get them at the Grove (EricSmith)

Dairy Queen at approximately 1:00, then onto the field (EricSmith)

Author's Note: We do not have a Dairy Queen in Petaluma, maybe we should get one! The boys really liked it.

Today was a day off for the Petaluma team. The boys had practice, then came to the hotel to spend some time at the pool and play a game called corn hole. What is corn hole you ask? It is a three by five foot box about

6-10 inches off the ground with one hole in it. The hole is about six inches in diameter. The goal is to toss bean bags into the hole and score for your team. If you get the bean bag in the hole, it is worth 3 points, if you get your bean bag to stay on the box it is worth one point. The first team to 15 wins. The boys played this game for a few hours switching off team members so that everyone who wanted to play had a turn. In between, they spent time in the pool and drank soda, lots of it.

Later that evening, the boys, the coaches and parents headed to dinner at the Old Corner Hotel. A better way to say it is, we took over the Old Corner Hotel dining room. I felt a little badly for the strangers in the dining room who could not possibly carry on a conversation with our very noisy, highly energized party of 50. The meal was nice. There was some homemade pasta, steak and other adult food, and the boys enjoyed the usual kid food including hamburgers, chicken nuggets and the like.

The boys and coaches were back at the Grove by 10pm in accordance with their curfew.

The rest of us returned to the Genetti Cave. It became obvious that we spent a lot of time there when the bartender would take our order and charge it to our room without even asking our room number. By now, you might be seeing a pattern. The perpetual baseball stress can be kept under control only with copious amounts of alcohol and late night baseball talk. We were learning to cope. Detox would come later.

Day 9: Thursday, August 23

The Day

Huddle Messages

From Williamsport

9:54am: Boys still sleeping (EricSmith)

Are we home or visitors? (Drewsdad)

Home (EricSmith)

Yes!! (BeckySmith)

11:26am: Boys are awake. Having lunch soon. (EricSmith)

12:25pm: Is there some sort of travel plan for the return trip home? We need to make sure there is a family member there to greet them (Drewsmom)

WTH is with the bad mojo??? Crimony!!! (Drew4Reds)

There are plans in the works. More info to follow when we know the day we are coming home (trev49)

Don't look past today... Period (Drew4Reds)

It would be nice to know how to plan either way (RachelBrandis)

There are plenty of people there to greet the boys. Enjoy the moment! No way to plan right now (BeckySmith)

First thing in the morning, we again secretly booked our return flight for Friday. I think we were at day 17 away from home. More than anything, we did not want to lose, but we were getting a bit home sick. If we lost, our plan was to get home as quickly as possible to get our life back in order and support Bailey in her first week of her final year of high school.

We took a mid-morning trip to the park to visit the official on site photo vendor. The photo vendor had told us at the parent meeting he and his staff would be taking pictures during the week, and we could come by and order from him at any time. Today was the day we set aside to review the pictures and make a buying decision. There were a dozen or so laptops set up in the photo vendor booth. We meticulously went through each game, the team shots and the opening ceremony pictures. It took us over an hour to review all the materials. Ultimately, we were disappointed to find that with Blake's limited playing time, there were not that many shots we were interested in purchasing. Maybe that was a good thing because the prints were very pricey. We purchased a few pictures, then checked that off of our list.

Bob and I agreed that we would come back to the photo booth one more time before we left on Sunday to review any additional pictures that might be of interest. One very important fact about the photos being taken was you could absolutely not buy them after the Little League World Series ended. If you did not buy now, you were out of luck. At first, I thought that was a bit strange. But, I guess they don't want to make the pictures available for purchase online because anyone could buy them and it might be a bit creepy if my son's picture was hanging on the bedroom wall of a random 12 year old girl somewhere in the world. Ok, I get it. It was good practice to restrict picture purchase to the event only.

The Game

<u>Huddle Messages</u>

From Williamsport

6:54pm: Let's Go Petaluma!!! (Ricardo)

Let's Go West!!! (Ricardo)

8:37pm: Can I come back from the restroom now?? (BeckySmith)

OMG Yes! (Ricardo)

On August 23, at 8:00pm, the Petaluma team decided to treat the fans and parents to a stress free game. Danny Marzo was eligible to pitch again and came out strong. The boys scored six runs in the first inning and won the game 11-1 after five innings based on the mercy rule. For non-baseball folks, the mercy rule means if you are ahead by 10 or more runs at the bottom of the inning (after 4 innings), the game is over.

In the game, Hance Smith hit his first ever grand slam. Not just his first grand slam of his Little League World Series experience, his first ever grand slam. Go Hance! Too bad Hance's mother, Becky, had left earlier in the day to return home to get her daughter situated in school. She missed the hoopla, but got to see it on television.

Quinton Gago followed with a solo homer and Hance followed with yet another homerun. The team put the game away with seven straight singles that scored four runs in the fifth inning.

Danny Marzo pitched a strong game, he struck out 11 batters in five innings with just one walk. He kept the Texas team off balance for sure. At one point in the game, when Danny was attempting to steal second base, the catcher made a throw and the ball hit Danny on the backside. That rear-end smack must have hurt, but Danny did not let it affect his outstanding pitching performance. Go Danny! I wonder what that bruise looked like?

That night in the Genetti Cave, we celebrated the win and with even more gusto, we celebrated the fact that the Petaluma National Little League All-Stars were playing for the United States Championship on Saturday, however, the Tennessee team had a big advantage. The Petaluma team, since we were coming from the loser bracket, had to play more games to get to the championship. Their starting pitchers were fresh, the same was not necessarily true for our team. Someone please pour me another glass of mediocre wine!

Also that night, it was clear that no matter what happened on Saturday, we were going to stay Sunday to watch the boys either play for the World Series Championship or for third/fourth place against an International team. For the final time, I cancelled our return flight (without penalty). And, we were clear to make plane reservations to fly home on Monday. No more guessing, we were committed to stay through Sunday. We booked our return flight or the final time. We picked the first flight out on Monday morning at 8:30am from Philadelphia, a three hour drive from Williamsport. In addition, we booked a flight for Bailey to head to Williamsport to watch her brother play in the US Championship game.

Huddle Messages

From Williamsport

12:00pm: I have a photo release form for the City of Petaluma. Please see me to sign. Need to get to Duarte. Thanks!!!

(UCLAHeather)

1:34am: Check your emails re: new passes/tics for Saturday's game. Go West!! (NicoleM)

Day 10: Friday, August 24

The Day

<u>Huddle Messages</u>

9:04am: Boys are awake. Planning Dairy Queen run after lunch and trip to reptile ranch. Then you can have them for dinner (EricSmith)

There is also a downtown street fair/market this evening that might be fun (EricSmith)

9:35am: Don't get rid of old VIP passes. Keep for new tickets (EricSmith)

7:39pm: Teddy is on his way out on the red eye tonight. (BeckySmith)

No way!!!! (Gagomama)

Nate says his curls are extra juicy (BeckySmith)

8:42pm: I am in Genetti bar and lobby with tixs for tomorrow. (NicoleM0

11:35pm: Here is the flight plan for the boys: flight # 1723, leave Philly at 6:00am to Atlanta, flight 682, Atlanta to SFO arrives at 11:19am (EricSmith).

This is for Monday the 27th (EricSmith)

Bailey and Becky Smith flew from home to Williamsport early on Friday. They would arrive in Williamsport just before 10pm. Bob and I were excited to show Bailey around the town and the field.

The Little League Park was closed on Friday. No games were scheduled in preparation for the championship games that were to take place over the weekend.

All of the teams were invited to an off-site event sponsored by the Little League World Series. Eric decided not to have the boys participate in the off-site event. Instead, the boys took a well-deserved trip to Dairy Queen then had a relaxing afternoon with their families. Many of the kids hung out at the pool playing corn hole, then migrated to a few hotel rooms to lay in a comfortable bed and watch a movie. In the evening, there was a "Williamsport Welcomes the World" street fair. The boys were not too interested, so they spent time in the Genetti Cave watching replays of their games. For the first time, they saw themselves on television. They were mesmerized. A group of 20-30 of us dined at the Brickyard that evening. The boys were back in to Grove well before 10pm.

I drove to the Williamsport airport and picked up Bailey, Becky and Nicole's sister Phoebe. All three were looking forward to tomorrow's game. They joined us in the Genetti Cave. The topic of conversation at the bar was the Tennessee team, our loss to them earlier in the week and our predictions of tomorrow's starting pitcher.

Day 11: Saturday, August 25

The Day

Yet again, Bob and I went to the Little League gift shop. We had received some texts from back home requesting some additional shirts. By this time, we had so much logo wear in our room, we were not sure how we were going to fit it in our suitcases to bring it all home. When we finally got to the front of the line to get into the gift shop, we were dumbfounded. The back left corner, which earlier in the week was covered in screaming yellow, was almost bare. We raced there and quickly determined the order we received could not be filled, there were no more shirts in the sizes we needed. Darn. I guess in a way, that was a compliment. The West gear was selling out. Our fans were making a statement. Go West. Also on that day, the store had a limited number of "Final Four" t-shirts that just hit the shelves. The shirt displayed: West, South East, Japan and Latin America. We bought one for Blake, Bob and our friend Sam Jacobs. As quickly as we could, we got out of the gift shop for the final time. When we exited, I made a point to look around at the crowds. There was screaming yellow everywhere. Who were all these people sporting yellow shirts and hats? They were our fans. How very cool.

The Game

<u>Huddle Messages</u>

From Williamsport

12:45am: Let's Go Petaluma!!! (Ricardo)

Let's Go West !!! (Ricardo)

Nice and early. I like it. (Drewsdad)

5:52pm: Hey everyone, tonight after the game the Genetti Hotel has offered to host a banquet for all of us. Boys included 7:30 dinner. (Gagomama)

The United States Championship game against Tennessee was scheduled for 4:00pm. The boys did not seem nervous at all. They warmed up as usual, danced with Dugout, and looked ready for a good game. The stadium was fuller than I had seen it all week. The press reported the crowd was over 24,000 fans.

In preparation for the game and large crowd, we were issued new parent and fan lanyards. Instead of just 42 seats, we were now allocated 63 lanyards with "golden tickets." Nicole once again, took on the task of allocating the lanyards. As I said before, the allocation was very tense. Nicole handled it with appropriate care and consideration. Our screaming yellow fan base was everywhere. We had a sea of yellow in the golden ticket area, and everywhere I looked around the field, there were pods of yellow shirts and hats. The team was very well represented.

Bob, Bailey and I assumed our standard seats in the parent zone. Before the game started, I turned to Bob and again whispered, "How did we get here?" Again, I did not expect an answer, and he just smiled. It seemed like the perpetual baseball stress was at its peak. I felt like my heart was going to beat out of my chest. The game finally started.

At the top of the 6th, we were down 15-5. It looked like the game was to be a blowout. The Tennessee team was hitting, hitting, hitting. We were facing our pitching challenges as best we could, but Tennessee was very strong. In the bottom of the 6th, in my estimation, 5,000 fans from both sides of the field started to exit the stadium. The Tennessee parents were holding up signs that said "FINISH IT."

Our parent section was very quiet and still. All sorts of thoughts were going through my head, "It's been a good ride. The boys should be proud of what they have done. This score gap is so big, how did that happen? Where is our hitting? We have made comebacks before, maybe in the bottom of the sixth we can close the 10 run deficit."

Then the never-give-up Petaluma team came to the plate in the bottom of the sixth. They started chipping away at the score. Bradley Smith hit a single hard up the middle. Kempton Brandis walked. Hance Smith singled to load the bases. This was getting interesting. Here was the team of boys we were used to. The Petaluma crowd re-found their spirit. "Pet-a-luma!" With every batter that came to the plate, we got louder and more emotional.

It continued. Quinton Gago hit a chopper to third, James O'Hanlon hit a blooper single to center. Cole Tomei drilled a double past the right fielder and scored two runs. Porter Slate brought home a run on a ground out. Logan Douglas got an infield single. "Pet-a-luma" got even louder and even more intense. Bradley Smith was up again and ripped an RBI double down the third-base line.

Kempton Brandis was at the plate for the second time in the inning. Petaluma was down 15-12. There was one person on base, and two outs. The stadium was in a quiet frenzy. It seemed that no one could believe what they were seeing. I was beyond nervous for Kempton. I looked over at Rachel, Kempton's mother, and she was standing, as we all were, with her mouth covered in anticipation. Kempton fell behind in the count 0-2. We exhaled when Kempton's bat landed an opposite-field homerun to bring the tying run to the plate. I turned to Rachel to show my support for her son, and she was visibly crying and laughing and trying to control herself in front of the ESPN camera. I blew her a kiss in support.

76

The parent section was jumping up and down, screaming, crying and laughing. The crowd went wild, all 20,000 of them. We were still winning the hearts of our fans and the respect of the viewers.

Hance Smith came to the plate. He hit the little white ball smack over the wall to the right of center field. The game was tied. I looked around at the Petaluma parents, we were all streaming tears of joy. What a site, what a thrill, what an emotional event, sixty four of us with bounding lanyards; thirteen families proud of thirteen boys, all in one spot, all wearing screaming yellow. The ESPN cameramen, the security people, everyone were wide eyed in amazement. They were chattering amongst themselves. "I have never seen anything like this. So exciting."

Now we were the team that needed to FINISH IT. Just one more run was all we needed. We fell short, and the game went into the seventh inning. Tennessee came back in the top of the 7th to score nine runs. In the bottom of the 7th, Petaluma was only able to score one.

The game was over with a final score of 24-16. The media reported both coaches' responses to the game:

> "I've never been in a game like that in my life," said Goodlettsville manager Joey Hale, who came into the post-game interview room sighing heavily and mopping his brow. "Thankfully we won, because, man, if we had gone home after having a 10-run lead in the final inning as losers, oh, God — whew, that would have been tough."

> "Asked what he told his stunned team after the game, Eric Smith said: "We haven't had a lot of time to talk about it. The message will be 'you never gave up.' All I've asked of them all year is to give your best effort. And they gave that. I mean, I never saw them quit, I never saw them think they were out of it.""

Bob, Bailey and I slowly exited Lamade Stadium. Strangers in screaming yellow logo wear patting us on the back saying "what a game." We smiled. We walked slowly to the base of the staircase that led to the parent tent and climbed all 2,000 stairs to the top. In tradition, we waited for the boys.

Amongst ourselves, we hugged, smiled, shook hands and exchanged high fives. We were part of a proud group of families and parents. Right then, we were all emotionally connected. Like one big family.

When the boys finally exited the Grove (we did not have to go into the parent, gnat tent), the media met them. They captured parents hugging their boys. The boys were jovial, gave interviews and were generally very upbeat.

Blake came to meet Bob, Bailey and I. We were off to the side of the media, just at the top of the stairs. We talked a bit about the game. Bailey gave him a big bear hug from behind and I saw it. Blake had his back to the team and was staring out at Lamade Stadium with a rim of tears in the bottom of his eyes. The tears had not dropped yet, but I could see that he needed space and time. I gave Bailey the motherly look of "back off for a second." She caught on, and backed away. I moved next to Blake and put my arm around him. We stared at the field lit up by enormous lights. The score was still on the board. And, it displayed the inning scores inaccurately. We had scored 10 runs in one inning, but the scoreboard could only display one character for each inning, so instead of saying 10 runs in the bottom of the 6th, it said "0." The final score was also there in big red numbers 24-16.

Then the tears came streaming down Blake's face. Unlike the uncontrollable tears he shed when he had not made the All-Star team, these were adult tears. They flowed down his face slowly. He did not try to stop or hide them. I said, "Do you want to take a walk?"

He said "No."

I said, "There is a lot of media here," he said "I don't care."

I stood next to him, with my arm around him and cried, too. I cried because he was crying. I cried because I knew in my heart the run was over. At that moment, the perpetual baseball stress was gone. I did not ask him why he was crying, we just stood there together with tears running down our faces.

After a few minutes, Blake cleared his tears using the sleeve of his jersey, and turned around to face his team and the media. A boy about his age walked up and asked for his autograph, he smiled and signed. I quickly wiped my tears and joined the crowd with him. My heart was so full of pride for my son.

Mark, the manager at the Genetti hotel, and his hard working staff, hosted a complimentary banquet for the families and team that night. The boys came in their jerseys, and we sat in a banquet room and celebrated together.

Dan Libarle, affectionately known as "Chief", Danny Marzo's grandfather, stood up before the meal to make the first toast. He did not move to the podium and microphone in the room, in his booming voice, he extoled the team, the great coaching staff, and then finished by saying he ends every toast with a group rendition of *God Bless America*" He started us off, and the entire room respectfully joined in song, held up our glasses and clinked.

The room was set up with eight to ten round tables full of happy people wearing screaming yellow. We enjoyed a nice meal, then Ricardo, Danny's father, walked to the podium for an after dinner toast. He used the microphone and spoke about how proud he was of the team and then complimented the coaching staff. Finally, he said, "I end every speech with the song *God Bless America*." He broke into song. "God bless America, land that I love...." The entire crowd exploded in laughter. The boys ran up to the podium, surrounded Ricardo and belted out the song for the second time that evening. We were louder, sillier and more relaxed during this rendition. I took out my camera and captured the team singing their hearts out in the front of their parents and families.

More toasts by parents followed. Each speech was from the heart. Finally, Eric came to the podium. He spoke of his respect for the team, their commitment to each other and the sport, their performance thus far, and extended compliments to his coaching staff. He also made some jokes about how much time they have all spent together.

After dessert, the boys returned to the Grove, and the parents migrated from the banquet room to the Genetti Cave. The conversation of the evening was about the game, the hits, the defense, and reminiscing about how the Petaluma boys just never give up. One parent even said, "It was good that we lost today."

I asked "Why would you say that?" "It is better to be playing for third place against Latin America than first place against Japan. It is better to return home as winners." She said.

Interesting perspective. I think she was right. We definitely had a better chance of beating the Latin America team than we did of beating Japan.

Day 12: Sunday, August 26

<u>Huddle Messages</u>

From Williamsport

8:57am: Home team (EricSmith)

Nice (Drewsdad)

The Day

We got up, put on our screaming yellow shirts and hats, ate breakfast and headed to the game. Bob made one last stop at the gift shop where he bought one more Little League World Series pin.

The Game

<u>Huddle Messages</u>

From Williamsport

10:32am: Let's Go Petaluma!!! (Ricardo)

Let's Go West!!! (Ricardo)

The game for 3rd or 4th place in the world, against Panama, representing Latin America, was scheduled to start on Sunday at 11am.

Petaluma defeated Latin America 12-4 at Lamade Stadium to end their epic All-Star experience on a winning note, in a game that lacked much of the intensity of Saturday's unimaginable classic.

It wasn't a world championship game, and it did not feel like one. The

Buhrer family was relaxed and I felt other families were too. At one point in the game, Bradley Smith was up. If Bradley connected one more time in the series, he would have set a World Series record, but the Panama team decided to intentionally walk him. Ricardo, Danny Marzo's father, hollered out, "We gave you the canal, and this is what you give us?" Bob and I cracked up.

At another moment in the game, the Panama crowd kept cheering something in their language that sounded like "row-sham-bow." Bob and I liked the sound of that, so just for fun, we started cheering it too, "row-sham-bow." Each time they chanted it, we joined it. I think it meant "strike him out," but we liked our interpretation better.

Logan Douglas played a large role as pitcher in the final win. Quinton Gago had started the game at pitcher for Petaluma, but he was relieved after he reported that his arm was hurting. Logan finished the game, striking out six, walking none and yielding just two earned runs in five innings.

Petaluma scored four in the first inning to build a 4-1 lead, added four more in the second to go up 8-2, then scored one in the fourth and three more in the sixth. The West team hit a total of five doubles and finished the game with a win of 12-4.

One last time, Bob, Bailey and I climbed the stairs from Lamade Stadium to the parent tent. Again, the number of steps multiplied. I turned to them both and said, "This is the last time we are going to climb these stairs." It was a bittersweet statement. At the top, we waited for the boys for the final time. I pulled out the World Series pin Bob had bought earlier to look at while we waited, then accidently dropped it. Damn, the pin broke. I guess I was wrong, that was NOT the final time I would climb the stairs to the parent tent. I smiled to myself, headed down the stairs and to the exit door of the gift shop. I explained my case to the attendant at the exit door, he quickly swapped out the broken pin with a new one.

On the side of the gift shop, for the last time, I looked at the team standings and took one last picture of it with my iPhone, then I noticed a large hand written sign, on a piece of cardboard, stuck to the wall with some package sealing tape. It said: "I wish to thank all the American people and the great fans of Mehta LLB Uganda for the great rooting of our team. My Facebook is odonghenry." He also included his email, which I will not reprint.

The sign was dated August 23, 2012. It was a goodbye message from the Uganda team manager. I took a picture of it on my iPhone too. Right then, I was very proud to be an American. I wanted to post a sign back saying how lucky we were to have met and learned from him and his team, but they were already on their way home.

Once again for the final, final time, I climbed the 5,000 steps to the parent tent. I turned around and looked down at the very normal, very non-descript steps and thought it was ironic they were so significant to me. I guess they represented the uphill climb to get to the Little League World Series, and the amazing thing was when I stood at the top of them, I could see the ultimate view of Lamade Stadium. Bailey and Bob were still waiting for the boys to come out. I joined them.

The team had their final lunch in the Grove, took off their jerseys and visited us in the parent tent along with the gnats. The intensity of the previous parent tent meetings was gone. We were all talking about going home. The boys had received their junior high school schedules and were comparing what classes they had with each other. Everyone was ready for the adventure to end.

Most parents were on a flight out on Monday morning. The boys were also scheduled to leave early Monday morning, but had to depart from the Grove that night in order to get to their very early morning flight. They would have to sleep in the van on the way. I reminded Blake to make sure he packed his bag well and not to leave anything behind. He gave me the "Really? You have to tell me that?" look. I guess in a way he was right. He had been on his own for 30 days where he had to keep track of his own stuff, follow directions, remember to eat, and get to bed on time. I did some self-talk in my head, "Too bad, I am your mother. I will never stop giving you direction. It is my job."

Later that day, Kitasuna Little League of Tokyo defeated Tennessee 12-2 in the world championship game, finishing 5-0. We did not stay to watch the game, but I suspect the West team had flattened the Tennessee pitching, and they were in a world of hurt against Japan.

Note that the overall record for Japan was 5-0. They played only 5 games in the World Series. Our overall record was 5-2. We played a total of 7 games and won as many as the Japan team.

World Series Championship Results

Win: Petaluma National Little League (PNLL)) 6 , Connecticut 4

Loss: Tennessee 9, Petaluma National Little League (PNLL) 6

Win: Petaluma National Little League (PNLL) 5, New Jersey 4

Win: Petaluma National Little League (PNLL) 5, Connecticut 0

Win: Petaluma National Little League (PNLL) 11, Texas 1

US Little League Championship game- Loss: Tennessee 24, Petaluma National Little League (PNLL) 16

Consolation game – Win: Petaluma National Little League (PNLL) 12, Panama 4

Day 13: Monday, August 27

Huddle Messages

From Atlanta

8:50am: on the plane in Atlanta. Boys are good (EricSmith)

Thank you (drewsdad)

On plane in Phil – sitting on runway/weather delay cannot take off. Looks like we will be late getting to Petaluma Go PNLL (Singly)

The boys boarded their flight departing from Maryland at 6:30 in the morning. They had one stop in Atlanta, then straight to San Francisco International.

Our flight, had seven of the families' on it and left from Pittsburg at

8:30am. We were scheduled to land in San Francisco 30 minutes after the boys landed. Our plan was to find the team in the airport and follow them home. What the boys did not know was once they landed, they were boarding a hummer limousine, with a police and a motorcycle escort by the Rip City Riders (a local biker club). We wanted to be part of the caravan into town.

After we boarded, we sat on the tarmac for an hour and a half, grounded by one of the Pennsylvania downpours accompanied by heavy winds. Tick Tock. We would not make it to greet the boys at the airport. We hoped their plane was delayed, too. It was not.

When we finally landed in San Francisco, over an hour late, we all turned on our phones, and the texts started coming in. The boys were already in route to Petaluma. There were pictures of them in the limo on Facebook already. We waited for our luggage, disappointed with the delay, hoping we could make up the time on the drive back to Petaluma.

Huddle Messages

From Petaluma

11:17am (PST): Boys have landed. Waiting for luggage (EricSmith)

Very grateful if some people can take photos/video of the arrival back in town! Thanks! (UCLAHeather)

12:38pm (PST) Just touched down in SF be there as soon as we can 7 families on board!!! (Singly)

They are almost to Novato on the 101 (UCLAHeather)

Seeing lots of CHP, cops and fire trucks lining up on 101 (Drewsdad)

Nope. We did not make it in time. As we drove home, friends sent texts. The boys were escorted back to town in style. The limo drove by Petaluma Junior High School where the school day was still in session. All of the students were temporarily dismissed from their classes to go out to wave to their classmates as they slowly drove around the school drop off circle. They did the same drive by at the high school. Then, the limousine headed to the Petaluma Fair grounds where several hundred friends and strangers greeted the boys in front of the press. I think there were two or three parents there, the ones who were smart enough to fly out the night before. We were totally disappointed that we missed the fanfare. According to the boys, it was a very special homecoming and their first glimpse of the support and sense of community they generated while they were away.

Blake hitched a ride to Hance's house on a police swat van that had been part of the escort caravan. Bob and I picked him up there once we made it back to town. Blake was so happy to see us. He was so happy to be home, and as expected, he was exhausted. The first thing he did when we pulled into the garage was greet his cats with big snuggle hugs. Then, he kicked off his shoes, went into the house and plopped himself onto the couch. Ahhh, home.

<u>Huddle Messages</u>

From Petaluma

4:20pm (PST): Did any of the kids end up with an extra iPad? (BeckySmith)

Later that night, when we watched the local news coverage of the boys coming home, they panned the folks who greeted the boys at the fairgrounds and there were three handmade signs that touched me. One said "You won our hearts." The other said "#3 in the World, #2 in the United States, #1 in our hearts." But, my favorite sign was small, written on plain brown cardboard with black letters. It very simply read "Never Give Up." Yes, that's the one that best described the heart and soul of the team.

6 - THE WILD WEST –
THIRD IN THE WORLD

The Warm Welcome Home

What we were not fully aware of while we were in Williamsport, was the effects the boys were having on our hometown and the surrounding communities, much of which I have only heard about from friends. But, apparently, what we missed was amazing. Every bar and restaurant that had a television was full of people watching the games. The local theater invited the community to watch the games on the large screens. It seems that everyone was rooting for our children. Facebook was full of pictures and support. There were signs of "welcome home," "thanks for the thrill" and so on in almost every local business. I had never had the honor of being the recipient of community support, and now I know what a wonderful feeling it is. I was so proud of what this town had done while we were gone. I was also so pleased that my son came home to experience the love and support of a community for something he had done. What a blessing.

The boys arrived home on Monday, and they all planned on going to school on Tuesday donning their jerseys. They had already missed four days of school. Twelve of the thirteen boys attend Petaluma Junior High School of the 12, 7 were 8th graders, the rest were entering 7th grade. On Tuesday morning, Blake got out of bed, put on his number 17, screaming yellow jersey, grabbed his West hat and headed out the door with an almost empty backpack. We had not been home to buy him any school supplies, so in his backpack, he had a pencil, a lunch and a sharpie. He asked me, "Why are you putting a sharpie in my backpack?" I responded "You will see."

When Blake came home that day, his lunch was untouched. When I asked him about it, he said, "I did not have time to eat today, Mom. I was busy all lunch signing autographs."

"Well, then it is a good thing I put a sharpie in your backpack," I responded.

Mid-week, we received an email from Troy Sanderson, the Treasurer of the Petaluma National Little League. His email detailed how to submit parent and sibling expenses in order to be considered for reimbursement from the community donations. We knew the community was making a big effort to fund raise while we were away, but were surprised to hear the total dollars that were accumulated. Out of respect for the league and the donors, I will not print the total amount, but it was big and it was generous. I will speak for all team parents here (hope no one minds), we received a substantial amount of money to cover most of our expenses and are so appreciative of everyone's contribution! From our hearts and wallets, "Thank You!"

The Parade and Community Dinner

The following Saturday, the boys were to be honored by the community with a parade through downtown Petaluma followed by a dinner with the Petaluma Little League community.

Prior to the parade, the team and parents were treated to a full breakfast at a local café. Then, we met in front of the bowling alley to prepare for the parade. Each boy and his family were provided with a classic convertible car and driver. The Buhrer car was a 1965 convertible Thunderbird in a pale, but shiny blue. It was lovely. On the driver and passenger doors was a sign with each boy's name and jersey number so the crowd could identify the players and family. We all climbed into our cars, with our boys sitting on the back of the convertible and proceeded to the parade line.

As we approached the start of the parade, I took a deep breath. There were hundreds, no thousands of people lining the street, five bodies deep waiting for the boys to ride thorough. Wow. I was in the back of the car sitting next to Blake and started giving him instructions on how to wave, and look at both sides of the street. He quickly tired of my instruction and said "Mom, quit telling me what to do." I decided he was right, I needed to just be quiet and enjoy the ride. So, that's what we did. The cars cruised in jersey number order through Petaluma. The parade covered maybe eight blocks.

From the car, I looked around at all the people watching the parade. They were mostly strangers. As each car drove by, the parade watchers would break into cheer and excitement. Occasionally, I would spot someone I knew in the crowd and wave a bit harder or smile a bit bigger to acknowledge I saw them. Blake just kept waving and smiling and turning from side to side to make sure to show his appreciation to both sides of the street. Bailey was sitting on the opposite side of Blake and she was waving too. Bob was in the front passenger seat grinning from ear to ear. I had no idea there were so many people supporting the team!! Another proud community moment for the Buhrer family.

Later the press reported that there were over 20,000 fans at the parade that day. How momentous, that those 20,000 people from Petaluma and neighboring towns came to share their appreciation with the Petaluma team. Such an honor.

Following the parade, the boys were delivered to a downtown park. At the park, they were ushered under a canopy to sign autographs. For over two hours, they signed, signed and signed some more. Then, local politicians congratulated the boys and thanked the community for their support. Just when I thought it was time to go home to get ready for the community dinner, the boys sat down in the shade and a line formed. One by one, people paid five dollars to have their picture taken with the team. The proceeds were proudly donated to the Uganda team. For over an hour, the boys and their coaches sat in their chairs and smiled over and over again for a very good cause. I was proud of my son for being a part of a fund raising event to benefit the friends he met from another country.

The day was not over yet. Still in their jerseys, the boys headed to the Little League community dinner with 500 attendees. The dinner invite was sent to all Petaluma Little League players plus one guest and people who had donated to the team. The entire meal was donated by various community members and was staffed by friends and family of the Little League community. Each player from our team was allocated 10 tickets for immediate family. What a party!

A San Francisco news station put together a video of the boy's journey to Williamsport through the eyes of the local fans. The video was about five minutes long and was a grand representation of the sentiment of the community banquet. Some league officials thanked the donors and the boys and coaches. Then, a music duo invited the boys to the stage and sang them the song they had written on their behalf.

Finally, Jonny Gomes, an outfielder and slugger for the Oakland A's came to the microphone. During the series, Jonny, who was raised in Petaluma, followed the games and shared his support of the team via social media. He was invited to the ceremony because of his connection to the town and the team, and his generous financial contribution. He did not come alone. He brought his brother Joey who was also at one time a professional ball player, and his teammate Josh Reddick, an outfielder and slugger playing for the Oakland A's. At the microphone, he told the boys how proud he was of their remarkable representation of his home town. He also made a humorous comment about the fact there were no San Francisco Giant players in the crowd. Everyone laughed. The boys were star struck. Jonny returned to his seat, amongst the rest of the Petaluma community and enjoyed the evening along with the rest of the 499 people in attendance.

Then, the party went into high gear. The disc jockey played music and parents and children took to the dance floor. The West boys hopped up onto the stage and showed us their best moves for over an hour. Memories and giggles for sure.

How Does it All End?

How does it all end? I am not sure. We have only been home for a little over month. The boys are still doing community appreciation events and signing autographs with wide smiles. As anticipated, the events to honor the boys are getting more sparse, and the signs of support in the town are getting faded and tattered from the wind and sun.

Blake has transitioned well into Petaluma Junior High School and after speaking with the other team parents, the rest of the boys seem to be doing well also. Blake was awarded his coveted iPhone per the promise from his

Dad. And, it is not broken yet. I still wear the lucky baseball St. Christopher medal, and I have no intention of returning it to Blake.

I put a lot of thought into my observations of this experience as a parent. Blake Buhrer learned more than my husband and I could ever have taught him. He experienced things some people never have the opportunity to in a lifetime. He learned how to be part of a high performing team, make friends with strangers, be humble, tolerate insanity, function without sleep, hunger for more, be a loser, and finally become a winner.

What did I learn? I learned I love my son enough to surrender him to the game of baseball.

ABOUT THE AUTHOR

Alexie Buhrer works at a technology company in Petaluma, California. This is her first published book. If you would like to connect with her, you can find her on LinkedIn and Facebook

www.ingramcontent.com/pod-product-compliance
Lightning Source LLC
LaVergne TN
LVHW021409080426
835508LV00020B/2518